TAKE YOUR
BIKE

Family Rides in New York's
Finger Lakes Region

by Rich & Sue Freeman

D1311022

Cover design by Michael A. Lynch, www.bookcoverdesign.com
Maps by Rich Freeman
Pictures by Rich & Sue Freeman

Cover photo by Andy Olenick, Fotowerks, Ltd., www.fotowerks.com

ISBN   978-1-930480-22-3
        1-930480-22-9

Manufactured in the United States of America

Library of Congress Control Number: 2006904107

Every effort has been made to provide accurate and up-to-date trail descriptions in this book. Hazards are noted where known, but conditions change constantly. Users of this book are reminded that they alone are responsible for their own safety when on any trail and that they use the routes described in this book at their own risk. Void where prohibited, taxed, or otherwise regulated. Contents may settle during shipping. Use only as directed. Discontinue use if a rash develops.

The authors, publishers, and distributors of this book assume no responsibility for any injury, misadventure, fine, arrest or loss occurring from use of the information contained herein.

If you find inaccurate information or substantially different conditions (after all, things do change), please send a note detailing your findings to:
    Footprint Press, Inc., 303 Pine Glen Court, Englewood, FL 34223
    or email: info@footprintpress.com

TAKE YOUR
BIKE

Family Rides in New York's
Finger Lakes Region

303 Pine Glen Court, Englewood, FL 34223
www.footprintpress.com

Footprint Press publishes a variety of outdoor recreation guidebooks. See a complete list and order form at the back of this book. We also publish a free, monthly ezine (electronic magazine) on outdoor recreation in central and western New York State. To sign up visit: www.footprintpress.com

Locations by Trail Number

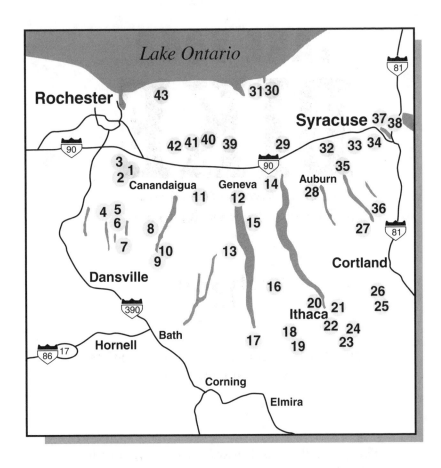

Lake Ontario

Rochester

81

43   31 30

Syracuse 37 38

90   42 41 40 39   29   32 33 34

3   90   35

2 1   Geneva 14   Auburn

Canandaigua   12   28

11

4 5   15   36

6   8   27   81

7   10   13

9   Cortland

Dansville   16

390   20 21   26 25

Ithaca   22 24

Bath   18   23

86 17   Hornell   17   19

Corning

Elmira

Contents

Acknowledgments 7

Introduction 9

How To Use This Book 11

Legend 12

Map Legend 15

Directions and Guidelines 16

History of the Bicycle 17

Types of Bikes 19

Safety 21

Bicycling with Children 22

Dogs Welcome! 23

Clothing and Equipment 23

Bike Racks 24

Rides in Livingston, Ontario, & Yates Counties

 1 Lehigh Crossing — Trolley Trail Loop 26

 2 Auburn Trail 30

 3 Dryer Road Park 37

 4 Hemlock Lake & Big Oaks Trails 40

 5 Kinney Creek Trail 45

 6 Canadice Lake Trail 47

 7 Harriet Hollister Spencer Memorial State Recreation Area .. 52

 8 Stid Hill Multiple Use Area 56

 9 Hi Tor Wildlife Management Area 59

10 Middlesex Valley Rail Trail 63

11 Ontario Pathways 68

12 Lakeshore Park / Seneca Lake State Park 77

13 Keuka Lake Outlet Trail 81

Rides in Seneca, Schuyler and Tompkins Counties

14 Frank J. Ludovico Sculpture Trail 90

15 Sampson State Park — Lake Trail 94

16 Finger Lakes National Forest 99

17 Catharine Valley Trail 107

18 Connecticut Hill Wildlife Management Area 116

19 Arnot Forest 120

20 Cayuga Waterfront Trail 125
21 East Ithaca Recreation Way 128
22 South Hill Recreation Way 130
23 Ridgeway Trail 134
24 Shindagin Hollow State Forest 137
25 Hammond Hill State Forest 140
26 Dryden Lake Park Trail 144

Rides in Cayuga, Onondaga, Cortland and Wayne Counties
27 Bear Swamp State Forest 150
28 Auburn - Fleming Trail 154
29 Howland Island 157
30 Cato - Fair Haven Trail (Cayuga County Trail) 161
31 Hannibal - Hojack Trail 165
The Erie Canal 167
32 Erie Canalway Trail (Port Byron to Jordan) 169
33 Erie Canalway Trail (Jordan to Camillus) 173
34 Erie Canal Park 176
35 Charlie Major Nature Trail 181
36 Spafford Forest 185
37 Onondaga Lake Park Trails (West Shore Trail, East Shore Trail,
    Long Branch Park) 188
38 Bear Trap Creek Bikeway 192
39 Canal Park Trailway 194
40 Old Erie Canal Lock 56 Trail 198
41 Erie Canalway Trail — Newark 202
42 Erie Canalway Trail — Aqueduct Park 205
43 Casey Park 209

Definitions 212
Trails by Length 214
Trails by Difficulty 216
Mountain Bike vs Paved Trails 217
Loop Trails 218
Word Index 219
Other Books by Footprint Press, Inc. 222
Order Form 224

Acknowledgments

The Finger Lakes region is blessed with civic leaders and private citizens who have preserved our heritage and built the trails described in this book for all of us to enjoy. Through the preservation of abandoned railroad beds and the development of trails in woodland areas, they're gradually building a network of trails that will someday crisscross our area. Each year, more miles are opened as the land is secured, brush is cleared, and bridges are built to span the many waterways. The rides described by the maps and guides in this book are works in progress. Every year, more is accomplished by groups such as:

Cayuga Waterfront Trail Initiative
Erie Canal Park & Sims' Museum
Friends of the Catharine Valley Trail
Friends of the Frank Ludovico Sculpture Trail
Friends of the Outlet
Finger Lakes Trail Conference
Ontario Pathways
Tompkins County Greenway Coalition
Victor Hiking Trails

We owe a debt of gratitude to these volunteer organizations. Without their hard work and dedication, we wouldn't have trails on which to ride or walk. We also thank the leaders of these groups for lending their time and energy to assure that the descriptions and facts about their trails are correct in this book.

Similarly, the foresight, planning, and action of our public officials has resulted in the paths dedicated to us bicyclists and outdoors enthusiasts. Kudos and thanks go to:

Cayuga County Office of Tourism
Cayuga County Park and Trails Commission
Cayuga County Planning Board
City of Ithaca
City of Rochester, Water and Lighting Bureau
Cornell Plantations
Cornell University, Department of Natural Resources
Finger Lakes National Forest Ranger District
Geneva Area Chamber of Commerce
New York State Department of Environmental Conservation (DEC)
New York State Canal Corp.

N.Y.S. Office of Parks, Recreation, & Historic Preservation
Onondaga County Parks Department
Sampson State Park
Seneca Lake State Park
Tompkins County Chamber of Commerce Foundation
Town of Dryden
Town of Ithaca Highway and Parks Department
Town of Jordan
Town of Livonia
Town of Ontario Parks & Recreation Department
Town of Skaneateles Recreation Department
Town of Victor Parks and Recreation
Wayne County Planning Department

People in these organizations directed us to choice trails, reviewed our maps and descriptions, supplied historical tidbits, and often are responsible for the existence and maintenance of the trails. They have our sincere appreciation.

Finally, a heartfelt thanks to Susan Domina, our proofreader. Her diligence significantly improved the guidebook you're about to use.

Introduction

"When the glaciers came they left in their wake a realm of gentle hills. And when the sun rose for the first time upon the new land, a spirit of the earth saw it and thought it so beautiful that he laid his hands upon the ground to bless it. When his hands were moved, the hollows left by his fingers were filled with water."

A local legend provided by the Finger Lakes Interpretive Center

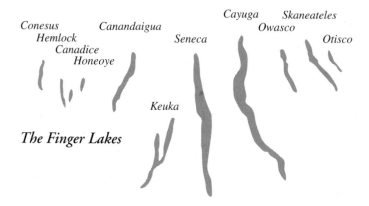

If you walk into a bike shop and ask where you can go bike riding and be safely off roads, you're not likely to hear many options. But, many trails are available in the Finger Lakes region; they're just a well-kept secret. Well, the secret's out! This book is loaded with havens to which you can retreat for a short respite or a long adventure. Choose the length and type of terrain to fit the ability of the participants.

We enjoy bike riding very much. It makes us feel great, it's fun, and it's inexpensive. What a combination! But, we don't particularly like riding the narrow shoulder of a busy road as cars and trucks zip by within inches of our bikes. That's not relaxing and certainly not fun. Biking doesn't have to be like that. Off-road alternatives exist that are much more conducive to a family outing or an invigorating adventure. You'll find them in this book.

The American Heart Association recommends 30 to 60 minutes of physical activity at least 3 to 4 times per week to maintain cardiovascular fitness. You're more likely to achieve this level if you choose activities that you enjoy and that are convenient. Biking is a perfect way to improve the

9

fitness of your heart and lungs. It burns calories too. Here's a breakdown of approximate calorie use per hour for three weight categories:

Person's Weight, lb.	Bicycling Rate, mph	Calories Burned per Hour
100	6	160
	12	270
150	6	240
	12	410
200	6	312
	12	534

You don't need a special (translation: expensive) bike to enjoy these trails. The only bike that isn't suited to an off-road venture is a road-racing bike. See the section "Types of Bikes" for specifics. The important things are to grab this guide, hop on your bike, and go for a ride.

And, why stop at bicycling? Many of the trails listed in this book are equally well suited to hiking, cross-country skiing, bird watching, in-line skating, and running. Enjoy them at various seasons and using various means of locomotion. Each visit can be a unique experience. CAUTION: If you venture onto the rural trails during the fall hunting season, be sure to wear bright colors (particularly blaze orange) so that hunters can spot you easily.

Many of the trails in this book were built by and are maintained by volunteer or community groups. They all welcome new members, especially anyone who is willing to help with the work. This is especially true of trails open to bicycles. We need to earn the right to ride on trails by participating in the development and particularly in the maintenance of trails. We encourage everyone to join a trail group and benefit from the camaraderie and service to your community. However, you do not need to be a member of the sponsoring group to enjoy any of the trails in this guide.

If you find inaccurate information or substantially different conditions (after all, things do change), please send a note detailing your findings to:　　　　Footprint Press, Inc.

　　　　　　303 Pine Glen Court, Englewood, FL 34223

or e-mail us through our web site:

　　　　　　www.footprintpress.com

How To Use This Book

The trails are clustered into three geographic areas, using county boundaries as groupings and working in a loop:

> Rides in Livingston, Ontario, and Yates Counties
> Rides in Seneca, Schuyler, and Tompkins Counties
> Rides in Cayuga, Onondaga, Cortland, and Wayne Counties

The trails range in length from a short 1.5 mile to 25 miles, with the average being about 6 miles. The trails are ranked by length in an index in the back of the book, so you can select ones to fit the endurance of your group. Many of the trails are loops. Converted railroad beds and trails that follow current or past canals generally are not loops. When you retrace the route, however, the return trip can often look quite different from your new perspective, even though you're covering the same ground. Alternatively, to add variety, there is always the option of riding one way on the trails and the other on the roads. Some of the trails can be joined to lengthen your ride, or the ride can be shortened by turning back at any point along the route or parking a car at one of the alternative parking areas listed.

The riding times given are approximate and assume an easy pace of 6 to 7 miles per hour. You may travel faster or slower, so adjust the times accordingly. Also, adjust the times to include stops or breaks for resting, eating, observing nature, viewing historical artifacts, and the like. You can easily stretch a two-hour bike ride into an all-afternoon affair, if you take time to enjoy the adventure along the way.

All of the trails in this guidebook are free and open to the public. If there is an admission option or any restrictions, you'll find them listed under "Admission" in the descriptive data for the trail. We also listed some of the amenities you'll find as you travel.

Legend

At the beginning of each trail listing, you will find a map and description with the following information:

Location: The closest town or lake and the county the trail is in.

Directions: How to find the trailhead parking area from a major road or town.

Alternative Parking: Other parking locations with access to the trail. Use these if you want to shorten your ride by starting or stopping at a spot other than the designated end point.

Riding Time: Approximate time to bike the trail at a moderate pace (about 6 to 7 miles per hour), adjusted for the difficulty of the terrain. Add to this "riding time," the amount of time you stop for breaks, sightseeing, or other fun adventures, to arrive at the total time needed for any particular outing.

Length: The distance from start to finish of each trek. Each distance will be designated as a loop, one-way, or round trip.

Difficulty:
(1 boot) Generally flat, a paved or hard-packed riding surface.

(2 boots) Could be rolling hills, a gradual grade, or a softer riding surface, so you'll pump those pedals a little harder.

(3 boots) Definitely hilly, but not necessarily steep. A more rugged riding surface.

(4 boots) Steep hills or a rough trail. You'll get an aerobic workout for sure.

Surface: The materials that make up the trail bed for the majority of the trail.

Trail Markings: Markings used to designate the trails in this book vary widely. Some trails are not marked at all but can be followed by cleared or worn paths. This doesn't pose a problem for the biker as long as there aren't many intersecting, unmarked paths. Other trails are well marked with either signs, blazes, or markers, and some times a combination of all three. Blazing is done by the official group that maintains the trail.

Signs – wooden or metal signs with instructions in words or pictures.

Blazes – painted markings on trees showing where the trail goes. Many blazes are rectangular and placed at standing eye level. Colors may be used to denote different trails. If a tree has twin blazes beside one another, you should proceed cautiously because the trail either turns or another trail intersects. Sometimes you'll see a section of trees with painted markings which aren't neat geometric shapes. These are probably boundary markers or trees marked for logging. Trail blazes are generally distinct geometric shapes and are placed at eye level.

Markers – small plastic or metal geometric shapes (square, round, triangular) nailed to trees at eye level to show where the trail goes. They also may be colored to denote different trails.

It is likely that at some point you will lose the blazes or markers while following a trail. The first thing to do is stop and look around. See if you can spot a blaze or marker by looking in all directions, including behind you. If not, backtrack until you see a blaze or marker, then proceed forward again, carefully following the markings.

Uses: Each trail has a series of icons depicting the activity or activities allowed on the trail. Jogging is allowed on all trails, as is snowshoeing when snow covers the ground. The icons include:

Hiking	Bicycling	Cross-country Skiing
Wheelchairs	In-line Skating	Running
Horseback Riding	Snowmobiling	

Admission: This line will only appear if there is an admission charge or some restriction on the use of the trails. In that case, it will state how much is recommended for the fee or donation, or what the restriction is.

Contact: The address and phone number of the organization to contact if you would like additional information or if you have questions not answered in this book.

Map Legend

Symbol	Description	Symbol	Description
✈	Airport		Water
—	Major Road	~	River or Creek
—	Secondary Road	♨	Waterfall
- - - - -	Seasonal Dirt Road		Park Boundary
======	Jeep Road or Double Track		Marsh
+++++++	Railroad	**P**	Parking
········	Power Lines		
••••••••	Recommended Trails	⟋⟍	Bridge
••••••••	Other Trails	⟍	Barrier
‖‖‖‖‖	Hike Only Trail	▥	Boardwalk
90	Interstate Road	■	Building
(104)	Road Route #		
(17)	Trail Post #		

Trail Blaze Colors:

Blue - Ⓑ	Orange - Ⓞ	White - Ⓦ
Brown - ⒷⓇ	Purple - Ⓟ	Yellow - Ⓨ
Green - Ⓖ	Red - Ⓡ	
Grey - ⒼⓎ	Violet - Ⓥ	

Directions

In the directions we often tell you to turn left or right. To avoid confusion, in some instances we have noted a compass direction in parentheses according to the following:

(N)	= north	(S)	= south
(E)	= east	(W)	= west

Some trails have "Y" or "T" junctions. A "Y" junction indicates one path that turns into two paths. The direction we give is either bear left or bear right. A "T" junction is one path that ends at another. The direction is turn left or turn right.

Guidelines

Any adventure in the outdoors can be inherently dangerous. It's important to watch where you are going and keep an eye on children. Some of these trails are on private property where permission is benevolently granted by the landowners. Please respect the landowners and their property. Follow all regulations posted on signs and stay on the trails. Our behavior today will determine how many of these wonderful trails remain for future generations to enjoy.

Follow "no-trace" ethics whenever you venture outdoors. "No-trace" ethics means that the only thing left behind as evidence of your passing are your footprints or tire tracks. Carry out all trash you carry in. Do not litter. In fact, carry a plastic bag with you and pick up any litter you happen upon along the way.

As the trails age and paths become worn, trail work groups sometimes reroute the trails. This helps control erosion and allows vegetation to return. It also means that if a sign or marker doesn't appear as it is described in the book, it's probably due to trail improvement.

Remember:

Take only pictures, leave only prints.

Please do not pick anything.

History of the Bicycle

For much of man's history on earth, he had two choices for getting around, either on foot or on the back of an animal (such as horses, mules, and wooly mammoths). Bicycles were developed to add another transportation option that multiplied human efficiency by a factor of approximately five. But the history of bicycles is very fuzzy. Sources often disagree as to the names of the inventors and the dates of their inventions. Leonardo DaVinci sketched a facsimile of the modern bicycle in 1490. It was way ahead of its time, and as far as we know, never left the drawing board.

DaVinci's sketch

Around 1790 a French craftsman named de Sivrac developed a "Celerifere" running machine, which had two in-line wheels connected by a beam. The rider straddled the beam and propelled the Celerifere by pushing his feet on the ground, scooter fashion.

Celerifere

In 1817 German Baron Karl von Drais added steering. Several versions appeared around France and England by the early 1800s. As a replacement for the horse, these "hobby horses" became a short-lived craze. The roads of the time were too rutted to allow for efficient wheeled transport.

Scottish blacksmith Kirkpatrick MacMillan developed a rear-drive bike in 1839 using a treadle and rod for the rear drive mechanism. However, he lived in the Northern British Isles where people and ideas traveled slowly, so his invention didn't spread. R.W. Thompson patented a pneumatic tube in 1845. Prior to this invention, bikes had metal wheels.

The French anointed Ernest Michaux "father of the bicycle," as he and his brother Pierre added cranks and pedals. Their Velocipede started a bicycle boom. The larger front wheel made it faster but less stable. The war of 1812 brought an end to the French bicycle boom.

Velocipede

British engineers were next to pick up the design and improve upon it by adding ball bearings, pneumatic (Dunlop) tires, wire-spoked wheels, chain drive, variable gears, and cable controls. Over a twenty-year span, the British brought the bicycle to its present form, thanks mainly to James Starley of the Coventry Sewing Machine Company. In 1885 the Starley Rover safety bike was born, returning wheels to a reasonable size and improving the bike's stability.

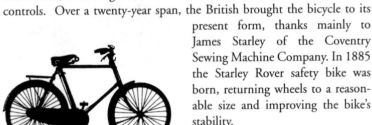

Safety Bicycle

In the early days, women's dress (corsets, pointed shoes, and voluminous skirts) limited their participation in this new sport. And, it wasn't popular with all men. Newspapers of the day railed against the "sorcers" or bicycle speedsters.

Types of Bikes

If you've shopped for a bicycle within the last ten years or so, you know that the choices can be overwhelming. So many types of bikes are available with unfamiliar names like derailleur, cruisers, mountain bikes, BMX, adult ballooners, and coaster-brake bikes. Gear speeds range from 1 to 21 speeds. To ride the trails listed in this book, you don't have to be an expert on bikes or have a specific type of bike. Many of the bikes housed in garages today (and often found at garage sales) are quite suitable on these trails. Let's review the major groups:

Road Bikes

Derailleur bikes are commonly called road bikes. They come in 5, 6, 10, 12, 15, or 20 speeds. The derailleur, a French word meaning "to derail," either lifts or pushes the chain from one gear to the next. These bikes are generally lightweight with drop handlebars, hand brakes, no fenders, a narrow saddle, and high pressure tires. Designed to be racing bikes and long-distance pavement bikes, their popularity boomed in the 1970s. Derailleur bikes can be used on any of the paved trails in this book; they are not suited to the non-paved trails.

Single-Speed, Coaster-Brake Bikes

Baby boomers like us have grown up with these bikes. They are heavy bikes with low-pressure balloon tires, wide upright handlebars, a large padded seat, and as the name implies, only one speed. Braking is accomplished by backpedaling. Tough, sturdy work-horses, these bikes last a long time and can take a pounding on the trails listed in this book. Because of the single speed, you may occasionally find yourself walking up a hill. (We do that anyway, even with our 15-speed bikes!)

Cruisers or Adult Ballooners

Internal-hub-geared bikes or cruisers have many features in common with the single-speed, coaster-brake bikes except that they do have gear shifting. The shifting mechanism is contained inside the rear hub and is activated by hand brakes and cables from the handlebars. They come in 2, 3, or 5 speeds. The term "ballooners" derives from their fat, low-pressure tires. They make excellent trail bikes.

BMX Bikes

BMX is an abbreviation for Bicycle Moto-Cross. These tough bikes are mini-ballooners with fat tires originally designed for trick riding both on and off road.

Mountain Bikes

Mountain bikes also called all-terrain bikes (ATB), became the rage of the 1990s. They offer the functionality of a road bike, with the durability of a cruiser. Mountain bikes typically have flat handlebars; heavy-duty brake levers; indexed, thumb-shift levers; wide, knobby tires; heavy-duty rims; and reinforced frames. They're designed to be light weight and strong, as an all-terrain vehicle. Mountain bikes are available in 10, 15, 18, and 21 speeds.

Safety

Regardless of age, everyone who hops on a bike should wear an approved, protective helmet. It's the law in New York State for anyone under the age of 14. Wearing a bicycle helmet significantly reduces the chances of a serious brain injury if you fall off of your bike. Unfortunately, every year nearly 50,000 bicyclists suffer serious head injuries. Many never fully recover, and often the injuries are fatal. Why take the risk when prevention is so simple?

The best defense against a bicycle accident is the safe and skillful handling of the bicycle. Some accidents are unavoidable, especially on trails where rocks, slippery roots, and woodchuck holes can present obstacles. Wearing a helmet while bicycling makes good sense. In the event of a fall, the helmet bears much of the impact and protects your skull and brain from the trauma that could result in serious injury or even death.

Three organizations have developed standards and test helmets to assure that they are effective in preventing head trauma. When selecting a helmet, look for a label or tag saying that the helmet meets the standards of ANSI (American National Standards Institute), ASTM (American Society of Testing and Materials), or Snell (Snell Memorial Foundation).

It's important that the helmet fits properly. It should sit level, cover your forehead, and not slide backward. Helmets come in many sizes; select one that feels comfortable and doesn't pinch. Then, use the sizing pads supplied with the helmet for "fine tuning" to achieve a snug fit. Finally, adjust the straps so that they are snug but not pinching. Now you're ready for an enjoyable and safe ride.

Courteous biking can help ensure that trails stay open for bikers. When you're around others, ride to the right in single file. Always signal before passing. It's easy for a bicycle to quickly sneak up on pedestrians or slower bikers and startle them. To avoid this, call out as you approach someone. A simple "on your left" alerts the person to your presence and lets them know which side you're approaching from. Ringing a bicycle bell has the same effect.

When you stop, pull off to the side of the path. Be conscious not to impede the progress of others. Stay on the trails. Do not create or use shortcuts, because they can result in added erosion to the area.

Bicycling with Children

Children love the excitement of bike riding. Add to that love new surroundings to explore, and you're sure to have a fun-filled adventure. Ensure a pleasant trip with these simple tips. Plan to take frequent breaks. Carry lots of water and some snacks. Play a game along the way. Read ahead in this guide and assign your child the task of finding the next area of interest. Let your child pick the next break spot. Take time to stop, point out, and discuss things  you find on the trail, such as beaver dams, animal tracks, and flowers.

You may have noticed that it's hard to find helmets small enough for an infant. There's a good reason for that. Infants under 12 months of age should not, and can not legally ride in a bicycle child seat, trailer, sidecar, or any other carrier. The fact is that babies are so susceptible to brain injuries that the risks outweigh the rewards. More than a third of the injuries to babies in carriers occur when the bicycle falls over while standing still. So, please wait until your child is a year old before taking him or her along on this enjoyable sport.

Once your child passes the one-year mark, you can begin using a child seat that mounts on the bike's rear wheel. Make sure that the child is wearing an approved helmet and is securely but comfortably belted. The bicycle should have spoke protectors to assure that the child's feet stay out of harm's way. The child seat should be high enough to support the child's head. Remember, when transporting a child in a child seat, your bicycle will require a longer breaking distance, will be less maneuverable, and will swerve if the child shifts suddenly. Specially designed trailers that you pull behind your bike have become popular for taking small children along on a ride.

Dogs Welcome!

With their keen sense of smell and different perspective on the world, dogs can make outings even more fun. Many times they find things that we would have passed without noticing. They're inquisitive about everything and make excellent companions. But to ensure that your "outing companion" enjoys the time outside, you must control your dog. Dogs are required to be leashed on most maintained public trails. The reasons are numerous, but the top ones are to protect dogs, to protect other hikers and bikers, and to ensure that your pet doesn't chase wildlife. Good dog manners go a long way toward creating goodwill and improving tolerance to their presence.

All of the trails listed in this book welcome dogs. Please respect the requirement that dogs be leashed where noted.

Clothing and Equipment

You don't need much more than a sturdy bicycle and a helmet to enjoy these trails, but here are some tips about clothing to wear and miscellaneous equipment to bring along. Shoes that tie or buckle are best; slip-on shoes could slip off unless they fit snugly. Sandals are not recommended. Sneakers are a good choice.

Dress in layers so you can peel down as your heart rate and body temperature rise during the trip. You'll probably have to put the layers back on when you stop for a break. We find it convenient to have a handle-bar bag on the front of our bikes for extra clothing and other items.

The one accessory that's mandatory is a bottle of water. It's easy to put a bottle holder on your bike or toss a water bottle in a handle-bar bag. Keeping hydrated is important even on a short trip.

Other handy things to have are an energy snack, a tire patch kit or spare tube and pump, a first-aid kit, a bike lock, insect repellent, sunscreen, a hat, a raincoat, and this guidebook.

Bike Racks

The first challenge in being able to enjoy the trails listed in this book is getting your bicycle to the trailheads. This often requires some sort of bike rack. Bike racks come in many varieties and many prices. You can spend well over $200 or pick up one inexpensively at a garage sale. Before you head out shopping, think about the following questions to help you select a rack to fit your needs.

1. What vehicle will be used to reach the trailheads?
2. How many bikes will you need to transport?
3. Do the bikes all have quick-release front wheels?
4. Are any of the bikes an unusual size or shape (for example, a small child's bike)?
5. Who will load the bicycles on the rack? Are they strong enough to lift the bicycles to the roof?
6. Will you need the extra security of a lockable bike rack?
7. Will the rack be specifically for bikes or will it also need to carry skis or other sports equipment?
8. How often are you likely to use the rack?
9. How much are you willing to spend?

No rack is ideal for all vehicles and users. The tradeoffs you make will depend on your situation. For instance, if you plan to use the rack infrequently, you may be willing to tradeoff some ease-of-use for a lower price. Here's some of the variety you'll find as you shop:

- Roof racks attach to the top of a vehicle. It's important to know if your vehicle has gutters or not when choosing a roof rack. Roof racks can be noisy from wind resistance. They require someone with strength and height to hoist the bicycles to the roof. You have to be careful not to forget that the bicycles are up there and drive into a garage. (We know this from experience!) With some roof racks, you can't open your vehicle's sun roof, however, they do allow full access to your trunk.
- Rear racks mount on the back of a vehicle with brackets and straps. They can scratch paint and can be hard to attach. Most limit your access to the trunk, but they are generally inexpensive, and you can load bikes quite easily.
- Hitch racks mount on the rear of a vehicle but use a trailer hitch as their main point of attachment. They're less likely to scratch your vehicle but are more expensive.
- Sport trailers are good for carrying many bicycles, but remember that you'll pay extra if you drive on a toll road. These trailers obviously require more storage space.

Rides in Livingston, Ontario and Yates Counties

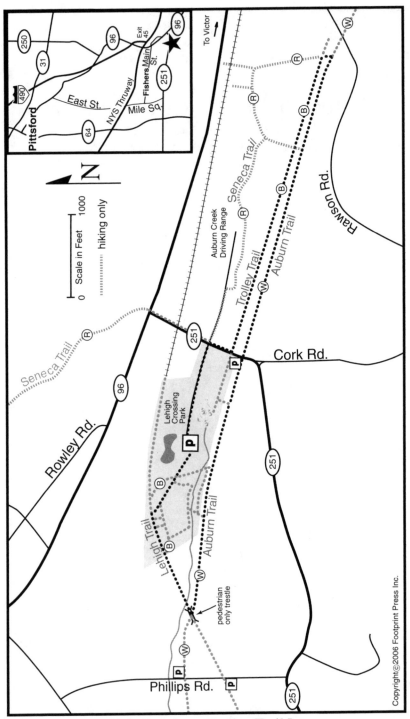

Lehigh Crossing - Trolley Trail Loop

1.

Lehigh Crossing — Trolley Trail Loop

Location:	Victor, Ontario County
Directions:	From Route 96 in Victor, turn south on Route 251. Cross over railroad tracks, then turn right into Lehigh Crossing Park. Drive back and park near the pond (no official parking area has been built yet). N42° 59.808 - W77° 26.368

Alternative Parking: 2-car parking area on Route 251 beside the Auburn Trail.   N42° 59.579 - W77° 26.215

Riding Time:	30 minute loop
Length:	3.5-mile loop
Difficulty:	
Surface:	Primarily hard-packed stone dust
Trail Markings:	Red blazes and diamond-shaped, red metal markers
Uses:	
Dogs:	OK
Contact:	Victor Hiking Trails
	85 East Main Street, Victor, NY 14564-1397
	(585) 234-8226 message line
	www.victorhikingtrails.org
	Town of Victor, Parks & Recreation
	85 East Main Street, Victor, NY 14564-1397
	www.victorny.org/parks.asp?cat=3

From Lehigh Crossing Park you can bike an historic loop, using the Lehigh Crossing Park Trails, the Lehigh Trail, the Auburn Trail, and the Trolley Trail. The terrain is flat to gently rolling hills. 2004 through 2006 saw major trail reconstruction on these multi-use trails. They were graded and covered with hard-packed stone dust, resulting in a wonderful biking surface. The Seneca Trail (shown on the map) is for hiking only. For additional information on the full Auburn Trail see page 30. For additional information on the Lehigh Trail see *Take Your Bike — Family Rides in the Rochester Area.*

Beavers inhabit the Lehigh Crossing Park area.

The Trolley Trail is on the bed of the old Rochester and Eastern Rapid Railway, built in 1902 to carry passengers from Rochester, through Canandaigua, to Geneva. Electric trolley cars ran this route until 1930. On the segment of trails you'll ride, the Auburn Trail parallels the Trolley Trail for several miles. Back in the early 1900s, this provided the perfect opportunity for steam and electricity to see which train propulsion method was faster. A race was set up with the R&E interurban trolley racing against a passenger train on the New York Central tracks. The electric trolley won and a party ensued near the cobblestone pumphouse in Fishers with a band, games, songs, refreshments, fireworks, and a "shooting of the anvil." According to J. Sheldon Fisher, "a blacksmith formed a two-inch-deep trough in an anvil and filled it with gunpowder. Another anvil was placed on top of the first anvil, and a long fuse was lit to announce the arrival of the trolley in Fishers. The blast was heard over 4 miles away in Victor." Relics from the race (a photo, the motorman's hat and badge and the railroad conductors hat, badge and coat) are at Valentown Museum.

Trail Directions
• From the pond area, head north on the wide trail.

- Continue straight, passing a blue-blazed trail to the right.
- Meet the ballast stone and grass Lehigh Trail, and turn left. You may prefer to walk your bike for a small distance through the stones.
- Just before the trestle bridge bear left down the connector ramp. Turn left at the base of the hill onto the Auburn Trail.
- Continue straight on the Auburn Trail, passing several side trails to the left.
- Cross Route 251, and continue following the white-blazed Auburn Trail.
- Pass an unmarked side trail to the left.
- Turn left at the second trail junction (red-blazed).
- Take a quick left onto the blue-blazed Trolley Trail. To your left you can see the Auburn Trail, so you're riding the path of railroad history.
- Continue straight to Route 251.
- Turn right onto Route 251, then a quick left into Lehigh Crossing Park to return to your car.

Date Enjoyed: _____

Notes:

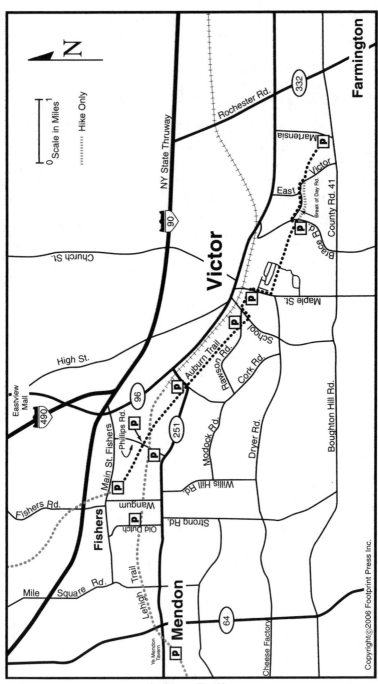

Auburn Trail

2.

Auburn Trail

Location: Fishers Road in Victor, to Martensia Road in Farmington, Ontario County

Directions: From Route 96 just south of the I-90 bridge, turn west onto Main Street Fishers. In the village of Fishers turn left into the Fishers Firehouse, and park behind the firehouse. N43° 00.508 - W77° 28.040

Alternative Parking: 2-car parking area north of trail on Phillips Road. N43° 00.119 - W77° 27.179

Alternative Parking: 2-car parking area north of trail on Route 251. N42° 59.591 - W77° 26.189

Alternative Parking: 2-car parking area north of trail on Rawson Road. N42° 58.830 - W77° 25.287

Alternative Parking: Victor Volunteer Fireman's Memorial Field on Maple Street in Victor. N42° 58.708 - W77° 24.622

Alternative Parking: West side of Martensia Road at brown sign saying "Farmington - Welcome to Auburn Trail." N42° 57.825 - W77° 21.980

Riding Time: 65 minutes one way

Length: 7.5 miles one way

Difficulty:

Surface: Hard-packed stone dust

Trail Markings: 3.5-inch white, rectangular, metal markers for "Victor Hiking Trail"
11-inch green-and-yellow "Victor Hiking Trail" signs at road crossings
Brown signs for "Farmington - Welcome to Auburn Trail"

Uses:

Dogs: OK on leash

Contact: Victor Hiking Trails, Inc.
85 East Main Street, Victor, NY 14564
www.victorhikingtrails.org
hotline: (585) 234-8226

The cobblestone pumphouse in Fishers, NY.

The Auburn Trail was one of the first trails opened by Victor Hiking Trails. This volunteer group was conceived by the Victor Conservation Board in the 1980s. The first organizational meeting occurred in September 1991, and the Auburn Trail opened in September 1993. The eastern section of the Auburn Trail was developed and is maintained by the town of Farmington.

The Auburn Trail is on the bed of the Auburn and Rochester Railroad, which opened in 1840. Charles Fisher owned over 1,000 acres of land in this area and operated a sawmill. "He donated a right-of-way for the railroad through his land. In exchange, he got an agreement that trains would stop at Fishers twice a day, that he would be the station agent, and that he would have the contract for supplying the railroad's lumber needs," per his great-grandson J. Sheldon Fisher in a dedication speech for Lehigh Crossing Park in 2001. At one time, the Auburn was part of the New York Central Railroad System, owned by Cornelius Vanderbilt, and it was the main east-west line in New York State.

Where the Auburn rail bed is not accessible in the village of Victor, this bikeway detours for a short distance on the old Rochester and Eastern Trolley bed. On your journey, you'll pass a train station from each of these lines. The trolley station will be directly in front of you as you cross Maple Street. The former Auburn trail station is in the Whistle Stop Arcade.

You will also pass through a massive tunnel built large enough for trains, under the New York State Thruway. At another point two former railroads cross, so you will ride under an old railroad trestle which was used by the Lehigh Valley Railroad. The trestle is now part of the Lehigh Valley Trail. A connector trail was built in 2005 to link the two trails.

Nature is plentiful along the way. Part of the rail bed is raised to overlook beautiful swamp and pond areas. Look carefully as you pedal, and you may be able to pick some blackberries for a quick snack. The trail abounds with birds, beaver, deer, and muskrats. Geese may even honk as you pass their pens.

History will also surround you. Be sure to watch for the old potato storage building and old rail sidings as you pass through Fishers. Stop to admire the cobblestone railroad pump house, built in 1845 (adjacent to the Fishers firehouse). It once pumped water from the creek to fuel the steam-powered locomotives and is the oldest cobblestone railroad building in the country (despite what the sign on its front says). To learn more about the unique cobblestone buildings in this region, pick up a copy of *Cobblestone Quest — Road Tours of New York's Historic Cobblestone Buildings*.

Concrete "tombstones" along the way were mileposts for the trains. One marked "S85" denoted that Syracuse was 85 miles away. A "W" in the concrete marker told the engineer that a road crossing was coming and to blow the train's whistle.

The Auburn Trail (before its resurfacing) heads under
the NYS Thruway through a tunnel.

Please stay on the white-marked railway bed. Other trails intersect this
path, but bikes are not permitted on them.

You'll notice the Lehigh Trail on the map. Like the Auburn Trail, the
Lehigh Trail was recently resurfaced and now offers an enjoyable bike ride
west to Rush, over the Genesee River and connects to the Genesee Valley
Greenway. To ride these trails, pick up a copy of *Take Your Bike — Family
Rides in the Rochester Area.*

Trail Distance Between Major Roads:

Fishers Road to Main Street, Fishers	0.6 mile
Main Street, Fishers to Phillips Road	0.9 mile
Phillips Road to Route 251	1.1 miles
Route 251 to Rawson Road	1.1 miles
Rawson Road to School Street	0.2 mile
School Street to Maple Street	0.6 mile
Maple Street to Whistle Stop	0.4 mile
Whistle Stop to Brace Road	1.2 miles
Brace Road to rail bed on E. Victor Road	0.8 mile
E. Victor Road to Martensia Road	0.6 mile

Trail Directions
• From the Fishers Firehouse, head right on the stone dust trail in front of
  the cobblestone pumphouse.

- Notice the old potato storage building on your right. Look for the water ditch from the creek that was used to funnel water to the cobblestone pump house.
- Cross Phillips Road. Parking is available here.
- Ride under the old trestle for the Lehigh Valley Railroad. A trail on the left connects the Auburn Trail with the Lehigh Valley Trail.
- Watch for beaver in the creek to your left.
- Cross Route 251 (Victor-Mendon Road). Parking is available here.
- A red marker for Seneca Trail is on the left. Bikes are not permitted on the Seneca Trail.
- The Seneca Trail (red markers) intersects again.
- Cross Rawson Road. Parking is available here.
- Turn left onto School Street. (The trail ahead turns into Seneca Trail and heads south toward Ganondagan National Historic Site. It is open to walkers only.)
- Just after the post office, the path turns to asphalt.
- Turn right to stay on the asphalt path.
- Cross active railroad tracks, then a wooden bridge.
- Arrive on Maple Street at the Victor Volunteer Fireman's Memorial Field sign. Parking is available here. Directly across Maple Street is the old trolley station, now the offices of Expidata Corporation. Downtown Victor and shops are to the left.
- Turn right (S) on Maple Street. Sidewalks are available on both sides of this busy road.
- Pass stately old homes along Maple Street. Pass East Street.
- Turn left onto the stone dust trail just after the sign for the Whistle Stop Arcade, passing a kiosk and bike rack. The former Rochester and Auburn train station and old railroad cars are on your left.
- Cross Ketchum Road. Ride through a wooded area.
- Victor Hills Golf Course is on the right.
- Turn left onto Brace Road. (The trail ahead, between Brace and East Victor Roads, is a narrow path through close trees. Bikes are not allowed.)
- At the stop sign, turn right onto Break Of Day Road.
- Turn right onto East Victor Road, and head uphill.
- Watch for a yellow-and-green "Hiking Trail" sign on the left, just before the power lines that cross East Victor Road, and turn left onto the trail bed.
- Negotiate some tight turns then a roller-coaster ride on a raised cinder bed.

- Pass a brown sign saying "Farmington - Welcome to Auburn Trail."
- Cross a bridge with chain-link sides over Mud Creek. (Notice the gorgeous view of the rock strewn creek to your right. In the spring, look for bluebells.)
- A cement pillar "S82" is hidden in the brush on the right (S) side of the trail. This told the train engineer that it was 82 miles to Syracuse.
- The trail ends at Martensia Road with parking available.

Date Enjoyed: _____

Notes:

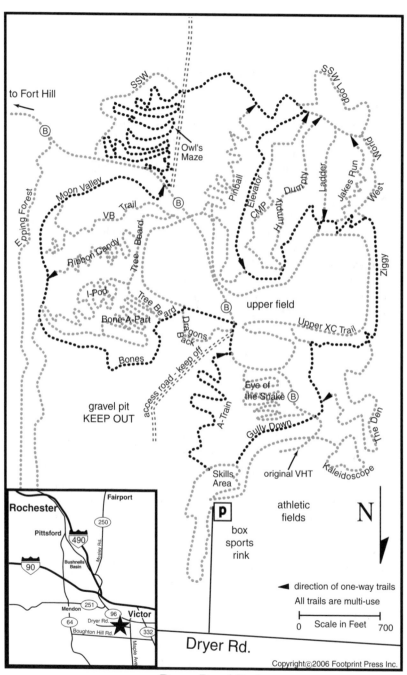

to Fort Hill

SSW

Owl's Maze

SSW Loop

World

West

Jakes Run

Ladder

Dumpty

Humpty

CMP

Elevator

Pinball

Moon Valley

VB   Trail

Ribbon Candy

Tree Beard

Epping Forest

I-Pod

Bone-A-Part

Tree Beard

Dragons Back

Bones

Ziggy

upper field

Upper XC Trail

gravel pit
KEEP OUT

access road - keep off

A-Train

Eye of
the Snake

Gully Down

original VHT

The Den

Kaleidoscope

Skills
Area

P

box
sports
rink

athletic
fields

N

◄ direction of one-way trails
All trails are multi-use

0   Scale in Feet   700

Rochester

Fairport

250

Pittsford

490

Mersky Rd.

90

Bushnells
Basin

251

Mendon

96

Dryer Rd.

Victor

64

Boughton Hill Rd.

332

Maple Ave.

Dryer Rd.

Copyright©2006 Footprint Press Inc.

Dryer Road Park

37

3.

Dryer Road Park

Location:	Dryer Road, Victor, Ontario County
Directions:	From Route 96 in the Village of Victor, head south on Maple Avenue (Route 444). Turn right (W) onto Dryer Road. Dryer Road Park is on the south side of Dryer Road, between Cork Road and Malone Road. N42° 58.375 - W77° 26.416
Riding Time:	40 minute loop
Length:	3-mile loop
Difficulty:	and (mountain biking)
Surface:	Dirt trails
Trail Markings:	Letter marker signs with difficulty ratings
Uses:	
Dogs:	OK on leash
Contact:	Town of Victor, Parks & Recreation 85 East Main Street, Victor, NY 14564-1397 www.victorny.org/parks
	Victor Mountain Bike Club www.victormtbc.com

One of the Town of Victor's newest parks, Dryer Road Park is still under development. Today it offers a playground, soccer/lacrosse fields, a box sports rink, restrooms, and a network of mountain biking trails. A blue-blazed trail cuts through the center of the park and heads to Ganondagan State Historic Site, with its network of hiking only trails (see *Take A Hike — Family Walks in New York's Finger Lakes Region*). The main part of Dryer Road Park consists of a field-covered plateau, rimmed by the Upper Cross-country Ski Trail. Off this trail are many winding, often steep, single-track mountain biking trails. They vary in degree of difficulty (beginner, intermediate and advanced), and some are one-way only (see arrows on map):

2 Boot Trails (beginner):

Marker	Name	Length (miles)
A	A-Train	0.31 (up only)
K	Kaleidoscope	0.2
G	Gully	0.2
X	X-country Loops	

EP	Epping Forest	

3 Boot Trails (intermediate):

Marker	Name	Length (miles)
B	Bones	0.2
BA	Bone-A-Part	
E	Elevator	0.22 (up only)
F	Fort Hill Trail	(up in sections)
I	I-Pod	
L	Ladder	(up only)
M	Moon Valley	0.37 (up in sections)
O	Owl's Maze	0.84
S	South by Southwest (SSW)	0.62
T	Tree Beard	0.22
V	VB Trail	0.23
Z	Ziggy	0.61

4 Boot Trails (advanced; one way only):

Marker	Name	Length (miles)
C	CMP (Check My Pants)	0.28 (down only)
D	Den	0.4 (down only)
H	Humpty Dumpty Downhill	0.18 (down only)
J	Jakes Run	0.34 (down only)
P	Pinball	0.43 (down only)
R	Ribbon Candy	0.32 (down only)

Recommended 3 Boot Loop:

- The trail begins straight back (S) from the parking area. At the kiosk, fill out a waiver form.
- Follow the A-Train Trail uphill.
- Turn left onto Upper Ski Trail on top of the plateau, and pass the access road.
- Turn left onto Tree Beard, then take the next left onto Bones.
- Bear left onto Moon Valley.
- Pass several trails, then turn left onto Owl's Maze (between VF Fort Hill Trail and an old dirt road).
- Turn right onto SSW.
- Pass Pinball to the right, then take the next right onto Elevator.
- At the top of the plateau, turn left onto Ziggy.
- Wind around, passing 6 side trails, then take a left on the seventh — Gully Down, which will lead to the parking area.

Date Enjoyed: _____

Notes:

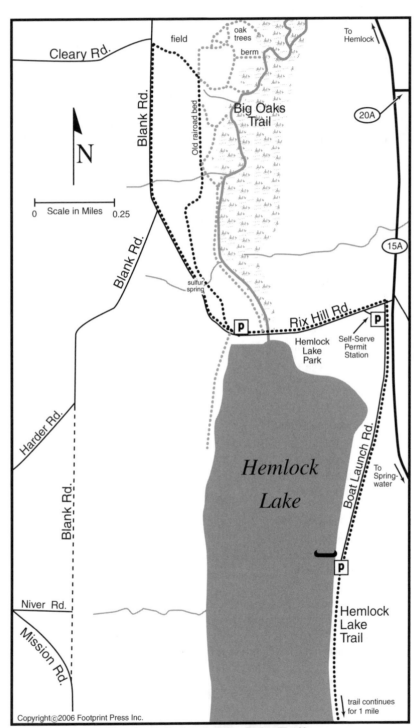

Hemlock Lake & Big Oaks Trails

4.

Hemlock Lake & Big Oaks Trails

Location:	The north end of Hemlock Lake, Livingston & Ontario Counties
Directions:	From Route 15A at the north end of Hemlock Lake, turn west onto Rix Hill Road. Take the first right into the loop. Park and pick up a permit at the self-serve permit area. N42° 46.745 - W77° 36.422
Alternative Parking:	From the permit area loop, head south on Boat Launch Road for 1.1 miles to park at the end, near the boat launch. N42° 45.834 - W77° 36.657
Alternative Parking:	From the permit area, drive west on Rix-Hill Road, cross Hemlock Lake Outlet and park at the trailhead on the right. N42° 46.669 - W77° 37.087
Riding Time:	1.5 hour loop
Length:	10.1-mile loop
Difficulty:	
Surface:	Dirt road, dirt double-track and woodland trails south of the permit station, mowed-grass trails (may be tall grass, may be wet) on Big Oaks Trail segment
Trail Markings:	None
Uses:	🚶 🚲 🏃
Facilities:	Portable toilet at boat launch, restrooms at Hemlock Lake Park (open May to mid-October, 7 AM to 10 PM)
Dogs:	OK on leash
Admission:	Free, but pick up a permit
Contact:	City of Rochester, Water and Lighting Bureau 7412 Rix Hill Road, Hemlock, NY 14466 (585) 428-3646

Early settlers tried to farm around Hemlock Lake but found the glacially scoured land ill-suited for farming. Many areas around the lake were too steep or too wet for growing crops. Eventually cottages sprung up along the shores of the lake. In 1872 the city of Rochester decided to use Canadice and Hemlock Lakes as a water supply. The first conduit for water was completed in 1876. By 1947 Rochester had purchased all of the shore-

Take a break at this bench to savor the serenity of Hemlock Lake.

line property and removed the cottages in order to help protect the water supply for its growing population. Although it was very difficult for the cottage residents to leave their land, this area is now free of the commercialization that is so rampant on the other Finger Lakes. Flow from Canadice Outlet Creek is diverted into the northern end of Hemlock Lake. From there the City of Rochester Water Bureau conditions the water for drinking and uses gravity to send it north for 29 miles via large pipes at a rate of up to 48 million gallons per 24-hour period.

Today, the Hemlock and Canadice Lakes watershed continues to be Rochester's primary source of drinking water. The watershed covers more than 40,000 acres of land, of which Rochester owns 7,000 acres. A second-growth forest prospers on the land and many abandoned farm fields have been reforested with conifers. Bald eagles are now present in the area.

To protect city property and the supply of drinking water, the city asks that all visitors obtain a Watershed Visitor Permit, one of the easiest permits to obtain. Just stop at the visitor's self-serve permit station located at the north end of Hemlock Lake on Rix Hill Road off Route 15A (see the map on page 40), or you can download it at www.cityofrochester.gov/watershedpermit.htm. There are no fees or forms to fill out, but the permit document details the dos and don'ts to help keep the area pristine, so it's important to read it. Swimming and camping are not permitted. Boats up to 16 feet long with motors up to 10 horsepower are okay. If you care to fish, the lake has salmon, trout, and panfish.

At the north end of Hemlock Lake, off Rix Hill Road, is beautiful Hemlock Lake Park, which has restrooms (May through mid-October), a pavilion with grills, and even a gazebo.

The exceptionally well-managed watershed area contains a variety of trees, including hemlock, beech, oak, maple, hickory, basswood, and white, red and scotch pine. You may see kingfishers, herons, ospreys, as well as bald eagles near the water. The relatively undisturbed forest along the trails is ideal habitat for several woodpecker species. Also, the narrow lake and forested shoreline create excellent sighting opportunities for spring and autumn migrating warblers and other songbirds.

The trail described follows dirt Boat Launch Road, then a double-track dirt trail, packed hard from City of Rochester, Water and Lighting Bureau truck tires to a stone bench with a panoramic view of Hemlock Lake. Then return to the permit station and head west along Rix Hill Road to the grassy Big Oaks Trail for a loop. A portion of the trail follows the former bed of the Lehigh Valley Railroad. Watch for an old foundation near the sulfur spring. Big Oaks Trail heads into a marshy area surrounding Hemlock Lake Outlet and can be very wet in spring. Late summer or fall is the best time to bicycle here.

Trail Directions
- From the self-serve permit stand off Rix Hill Road, begin your southward journey on the paved loop.
- Turn right (S) onto the seasonal dirt road leading to the boat launch.
- Pass the boat launch and portable toilet at 1.1 miles. Continue straight past the grey metal gate.
- At 2.8 miles the double-track ends. Leave your bike here, or walk it over the culvert and onto a narrow path through the woods.
- In another 0.1 mile you'll reach a stone bench overlooking Hemlock Lake, the perfect place for a contemplative break.
- Reverse direction to follow the double-track and seasonal road back to the self-serve permit stand at 5.9 miles.
- Turn left and follow Rix Hill Road.
- Pass the water filtration plant, then the entrance to Hemlock Lake Park at 6.2 miles.
- Cross the bridge over Hemlock Lake Outlet.

- In another 0.1 mile, turn right through the trail parking area and pass a silver metal gate. This is marked with a green-and-white sign that reads "Hemlock-Canadice Watershed."
- You're now on a grass trail (sporadically mowed).
- Cross two small streams.
- At 7.2 miles (0.7 miles on this trail) the first loop trail heads off to the right. (You can take this 0.25-mile loop if you wish.)
- The return of the side loop trail meets the main trail at 7.4 miles.
- Pass a third trail to the right. (This is the start of a loop through a field.)
- Pass a forth trail to the right. (This is the end of the field loop.)
- Continue along the edge of a field.
- Reach Blank Road at 7.7 miles. Turn left to ride south on Blank Road.
- Bear left onto Rix Hill Road to return to the self-serve permit station.

Date Enjoyed: _____

Notes:

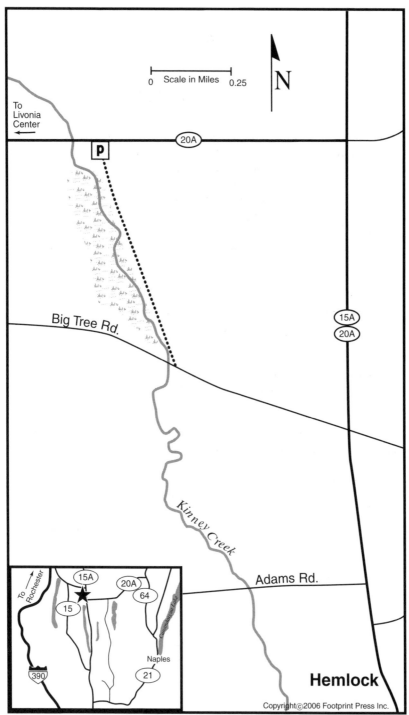

Kinney Creek Trail

5.

Kinney Creek Trail

Location:	Route 20A, Livonia Center, Livingston County
Directions:	From Route 15A, head west on Route 20A for 0.8 mile. Turn left at a bright blue metal building (7074 Route 20A, Livonia Highway Barns) and park on the left side in front of the chain-link fence. N42° 49.278 - W77° 37.666
Riding Time:	15 minutes round trip
Length:	1.5 mile round trip
Difficulty:	
Surface:	Dirt trail
Trail Markings:	None
Uses:	
Dogs:	OK on leash
Contact:	Town of Livonia 36 Commercial Street, Livonia, NY 14487 (585) 346-3100

Built in 1998, this former railroad bed is now a narrow 0.75-mile long trail through trees and brush. Perfect for a quick escape into the woods.

Trail Directions

- Pass through the gate labeled "Enter here for Kinney Creek Trail" and head straight back.
- Follow the trail to Big Tree Road, then turn around and ride back to Route 20A.

Date Enjoyed: _____

Notes:

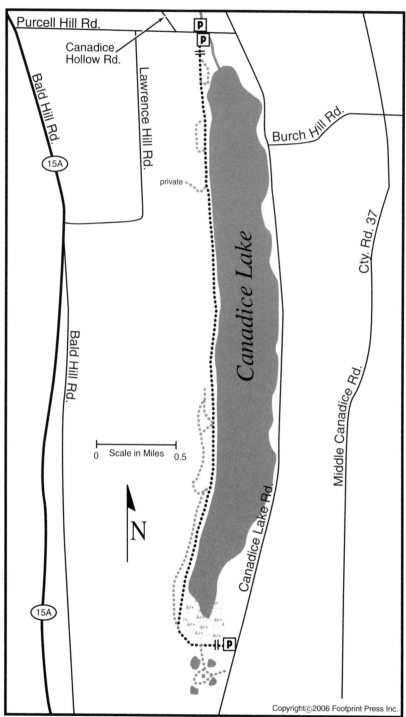

Purcell Hill Rd.

Canadice
Hollow Rd.

Bald Hill Rd.

15A

Lawrence Hill Rd.

Bald Hill Rd.

private

Canadice Lake

Burch Hill Rd.

Cty. Rd. 37

Middle Canadice Rd.

Canadice Lake Rd.

Scale in Miles
0   0.5

N

15A

Canadice Lake Trails

6.

Canadice Lake Trail

Location:	West side of Canadice Lake, Ontario County
Directions:	From Route 15A, turn east onto Purcell Hill Road. Find a dirt parking area on the north side, midway between Canadice Hollow Road and Canadice Lake Road. Additional parking is available at the beginning of the trail. N42° 44.621 - W77° 34.416
Alternative Parking:	A small pull-off along Canadice Lake Road, 3.7 miles south of Purcell Hill Road on west side of road (lake side), near a blue gate. N42° 41.513 - W77° 34.144
Riding Time:	70 minutes round trip
Length:	8.1 miles round trip
	9.0 miles total (including side trails)
Difficulty:	On the trail parallel to the lake.
	The loops up the hillside require technical mountain biking and are not currently well marked.
Surface:	Gravel and grass double-track
Trail Markings:	Green-and-white signs labeled with hiker silhouettes and "Hemlock Canadice Watershed"
Uses:	
Dogs:	OK on leash
Admission:	Free, but pick up a permit
Contact:	City of Rochester, Water and Lighting Bureau 7412 Rix Hill Road, Hemlock, NY 14466 (585) 428-3646

Early settlers tried to farm around Canadice Lake but found the glacially scoured land ill-suited for farming. Many areas around the lake were too steep or too wet for growing crops. Eventually, the Canadice Lake shore became rimmed with cottages. However, in 1872 the city of Rochester decided to use Canadice and Hemlock Lakes as a water supply. The first conduit for water was completed in 1876. By 1947 Rochester had purchased all of the shoreline property and removed the cottages in order to

A tree-shaded trail parallels Canadice Lake.

help protect the water supply for its growing population. Although it was very difficult for the cottage residents to leave their land, this area is now free of the commercialization that is so rampant on the other Finger Lakes. Ninety-foot-deep Canadice Lake is the smallest of the Finger Lakes, but it has the highest elevation, at 1,096 feet, one of the reasons it is such a good water supply for the city. Flow from Canadice Outlet Creek is diverted into the northern end of Hemlock Lake. From there the City of Rochester Water Bureau conditions the water for drinking and uses gravity to send it north for 29 miles via large pipes at a rate of up to 48 million gallons per 24-hour period.

Today, the Hemlock and Canadice Lakes watershed continues to be Rochester's primary source of drinking water. The watershed covers more than 40,000 acres of land, of which Rochester owns 7,000 acres. A second-growth forest prospers on the land and many abandoned farm fields have been reforested with conifers. Bald eagles are now present in the area.

To protect city property and the supply of drinking water, the city asks that all visitors obtain a Watershed Visitor Permit, one of the easiest permits to obtain. Just stop at the visitor's self-serve, permit station located at the north end of Hemlock Lake on Rix Hill Road off Route 15A (see the maps on page 40 or 47) or download it at www.cityofrochester.gov/watershedpermit.htm. There are no fees or forms to fill out, but the permit document details the dos and don'ts to help keep

Rest at this bench to enjoy a view of the south end of Canadice Lake.

the area pristine, so it's important to read it. Swimming and camping are not permitted. Boats up to 16 feet long with motors up to 10 horsepower are okay.

The Canadice Lake Trail, an abandoned town road, meanders back and forth through oak, maple, tulip poplar, and conifer trees, but is never very far from the lake. See if you can spot the old cottage foundations along the way.

Trail Directions
- From the parking area, head south past the silver gate.
- Pass a side loop to the left (level and easy biking), then multiple trails to your right. (You can bike these, but they are steep dirt paths with sharp bends. Only attempt them with a mountain bike.)
- At the end of the lake, the trail turns left (E) onto gravel.
- At the bench you have a choice. You can continue straight and soon arrive at a blue, gated trail entrance off of Canadice Lake Road (N42º 41.513 - W77º 144), or you can turn right to explore a circle trail with a bench in the center. Off the circle is another trail that also takes you to Canadice Lake Road (N42º 41.352 - W77º 34.189).

Date Enjoyed: _____
Notes:

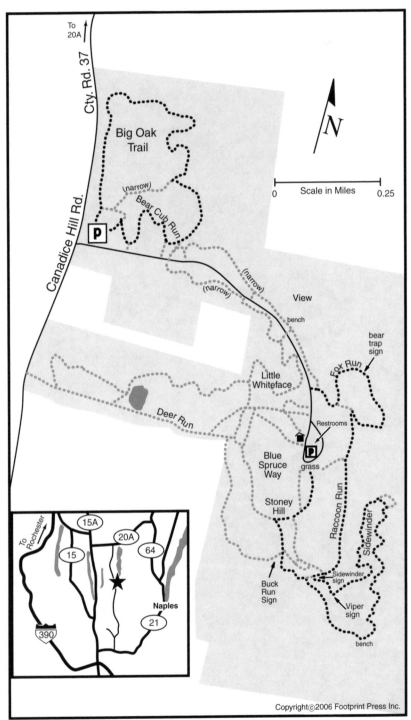

Harriet Hollister Spencer Memorial State Recreation Area

7.

Harriet Hollister Spencer Memorial State Recreation Area

Location: South of Honeoye Lake, Ontario County

Directions: From Route 390, head east on Route 20A through Livonia. Continue east past Route 15A. Turn south on Canadice Hill Road County Road 37). Pass Ross Road. Canadice Hill Road will turn to gravel. Turn left at the sign "Harriet Hollister Spencer Memorial State Recreation Area" and park in the parking area on the left. N42° 41.673 - W77° 31.507

Alternative Parking: Along the loop at the end of the park road. N42° 41.349 - W77° 30.793

Length: Over 10 miles of trails

Difficulty: (mountain biking)

Surface: Dirt trails

Trail Markings: Some cross-country ski trail signs (blue squares, black diamonds) and some brown and yellow trail-name signs.

Uses:

Dogs: OK on leash

Contact: N.Y.S. Office of Parks, Recreation and Historic Preservation
Stony Brook State Park
10820 Route 36 South, Dansville, NY 14437
(585) 335-8111

High in the hills, between Canadice Lake and Honeoye Lake, this area is treasured by cross-country skiers because it often has snow when the surrounding area doesn't. The trails in this park are constructed, maintained, and groomed in winter by volunteers from the N.Y.S. Section 5 Ski League. The rest of the year, the trails are lesser used and are a wonderland for hikers and off-road bikers.

A trail parallel to the park road offers a grand view of Honeoye Lake in the valley. A bench labeled "A favorite place of Todd Ewers" is available to sit and savor the view.

A view of Honeoye Lake from the trails in Harriet Hollister.

Within the woods you'll follow 8-foot wide hard-packed dirt trails. Sometimes narrow trails veer off as shortcuts or deer paths, but stay on the wide trails.

Big Oak and Bear Cub Loop
Riding Time: 20 minute loop
Length: 1.9-mile loop (darkened trail)

The Big Oak and Bear Cub Trail loop rambles through deep woods and is shady and cool on a hot day. We once watched a family of baby raccoons play along the trail. The southeast section of this loop is steep.

Trail Directions
- From the parking area near Canadice Hill Road, head north on the trail.
- Bear left on Big Oak Trail past a blue, "more difficult" cross-country ski sign. (Bear Cub Run is to the right.)
- Follow the trail around, staying on the main trail.
- Toward the top of a hill, bear right, then take a quick right turn. You're now on Bear Cub Run. (Straight leads to the park road.)
- At the "T," turn left to return to the parking area.

Date Enjoyed: _____

Notes:

Fox Run - Raccoon Run - Sidewinder Loop
Riding Time: 30 minute loop
Length: 2.6-mile loop (darkened trail)

Take a longer ride through these pristine woods by combining several trails. The trails are poorly marked, but a few signs along the way can act as waymarkers.

Trail Directions
• Park along the loop at the end of the park road.
• Ride back down the road to find the first trail to the right (E), labeled Fox Run.
• Follow Fox Run as it winds, passing a "bear trap" sign.
• When the trail meets Raccoon Run, turn left.
• Take the first left onto Sidewinder at the sign "Sidewinder - one way" (N42º 41.123 - W77º 30.723). As the name implies, this trail will wind.
• Pass a "viper" sign at N42º 41.092 - W77º 30.628.
• Pass a bench at the base of a steep hill at N42º 41.022 - W77º 30.548.
• At the "T" turn left.
• Continue straight through a trail junction.
• At the next "T," turn right.
• Pass a trail to the right, then one to the left. Follow the trail downhill to a grassy area.
• Cross the grass to return to the parking loop.

Date Enjoyed: _____

Notes:

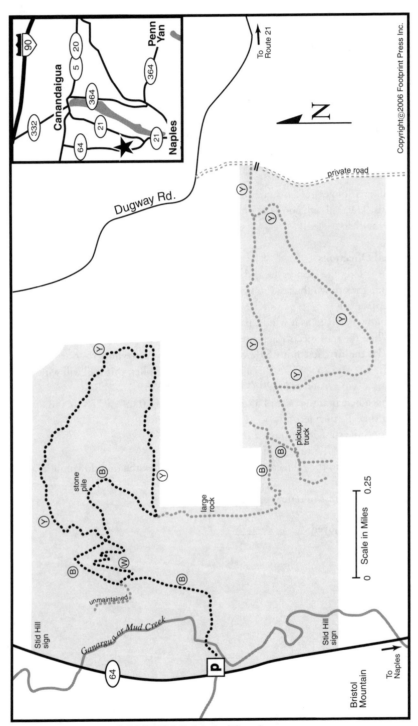

Stid Hill Multiple Use Area

8.

Stid Hill Multiple Use Area

Location:	Bristol, Ontario County
Directions:	Take Route 64 south from Route 5 & 20. The Stid Hill parking area is 1.7 miles south of Dugway Road (bottom of the hill), just past the D.E.C. "Stid Hill" sign. N42° 45.930 - W77° 24.364
Alternative Parking:	Along Dugway Road, 2.0 miles from Route 64 (top of the hill), where a square yellow sign on a tree up a steep dirt road reads "Unauthorized Vehicles Prohibited" Below it is a round, yellow D.E.C. marker. N42° 45.986 - W77° 22.739
Riding Time:	40 minute loop
Length:	3.4-mile loop (darkened trail)
	6.5 miles total trails
Difficulty:	🥾🥾🥾🥾 (mountain biking trail)
Surface:	Dirt trail
Trail Markings:	3"round, yellow D.E.C. markers, colored blazes
Uses:	🚶 🚴 🏃
Dogs:	OK
Admission:	Free, open June 1 through late fall
Contact:	New York State D.E.C.
	6274 East Avon-Lima Road, Avon, NY 14414
	(585) 226-2466
	Rochester Bicycling Club
	PO Box 10100, Rochester, NY 14610
	www.rochesterbicyclingclub.org

Stid Hill, as the name implies, sits on the side of a hill. The area, opposite Bristol Mountain Ski Resort, is comprised of 3 tracts of land totalling 740 acres. At one time, Stid Hill was productive sheep and cattle grazing land. The livestock are gone. Left behind are steep hills, ravines, gullies, gorges, woods, and open fields that provide varied habitat for wildlife.

Included in the wildlife you'll find on Stid Hill are mountain biking enthusiasts. Members of the Rochester Bicycling Club and the National Mountain Bike Patrol created, maintain, and patrol the trails you'll ride. The trails are in great shape, and we thoroughly enjoyed biking here. The trail directions describe a loop starting from and returning to Route 64. For a long downhill run, start off Dugway Road and head down to Route 64.

Trail Directions

- From the Route 64 parking area, follow the mowed-grass trail, and cross a bridge over Ganargua Creek.
- At the white trail, turn right to head uphill.
- Continue straight onto the yellow trail.
- At the blue trail, turn right.
- Follow the blue trail downhill, all the way to the parking area.

Date Enjoyed: _____

Notes:

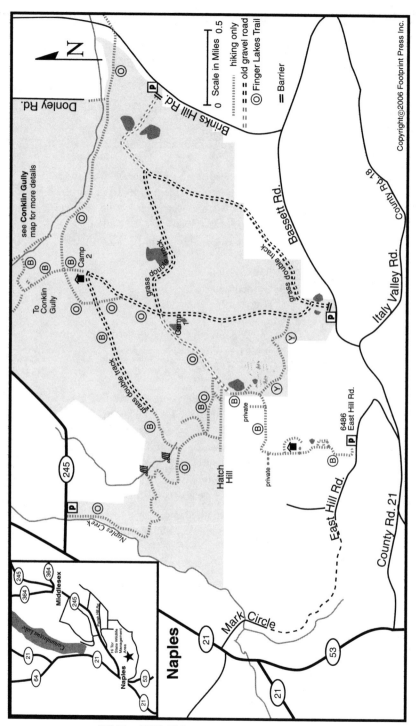

Hi Tor Wildlife Management Area

9.

Hi Tor Wildlife Management Area

Location: Naples, south end of Canandaigua Lake, Ontario and
                              Yates Counties
Directions: From Naples, head south on Route 21, then south on
                              Route 53. Turn left onto County Road 21. Turn left
                              onto Bassett Road, and watch left for the trailhead
                              parking area. N42º 35.986 - W77º 21.801
Alternative Parking: Brinks Hill Road N42º 37.057 - W77º 20.044
Hiking Time: 1.3 hour loop
Length: 7.4-mile loop (darkened trails)
                              17 miles total trails
Difficulty:

Surface: Gravel road, double-track, and mowed-grass paths
Trail Markings: Some trails are color blazed
Uses:

                              (Note, the orange-blazed Finger Lakes Trail and some
                              blue-blazed side trails are for hiking only)
Dogs: OK on leash
Contact: Hi Tor Wildlife Management Area
                              N.Y.S. Department of Environmental Conservation
                              6274 East Avon-Lima Road, Avon, NY 14414
                              (585) 226-2466 www.dec.state.ny.us

                              Finger Lakes Trail Conference
                              6111 Visitor Center Rd., Mt. Morris, NY 14510
                              (585) 658-9320 www.fingerlakestrail.org

Hi Tor (sometimes spelled High Tor) is an old English word meaning high, craggy hill or peak. You'll agree with the "high" part as you climb steeply up Hatch Hill. The crags are the sharp gullies and eroded cliffs which cross this hill, making it scenic and physically challenging.

Hi Tor Wildlife Management Area is a complex of 6,100 acres of hills, woods, and marshlands managed by the Department of Environmental Conservation (D.E.C.).

A view of Canandaigua Lake from Hi Tor.

Prepare for a strenuous climb as you begin this ride. Every trail points uphill to Camp 2. The bikeable trails are old gravel roads. Some are still gravel, some have evolved to grassy double-track lanes. The maps shows only these major old road trails and the currently used hiking trails. Other trails exist in Hi Tor but they are swaths through the woods or fields that rarely get mowed and can be a challenge to find.

Camping is not allowed in the Hi Tor Wildlife Management Area except by organized groups during non-hunting seasons with a written permit from the D.E.C. Regional Wildlife Manager in Avon.

Trail Directions
- From the parking area off Bassett Road, head north past metal gates on an old gravel road.
- It will begin gradually and build to a steep slope.
- Continue north staying on the gravel road until it ends at Camp 2. Look for the view to Canandaigua Lake in the valley far below.
- Turn left and follow a wide, blue-blazed double-track downhill, south-west until the old road ends.
- Turn around and head back uphill to Camp 2
- Head back south on the old road you originally followed uphill.

•This time where the orange-blazed trail turns, head left on a grassy double-track.
•Watch for another grassy double-track to the right, and turn right to head
downhill back to the Bassett Road parking area.

Date Enjoyed: _____

Notes:

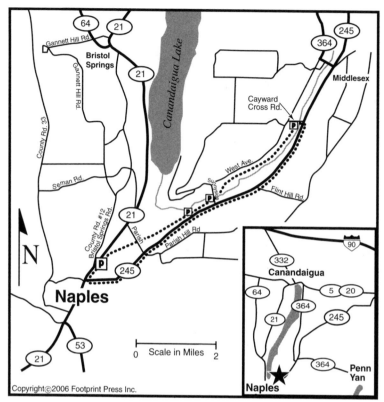

Middlesex Valley Rail Trail

10.

Middlesex Valley Rail Trail

Location:	Hi Tor area, Naples, Yates County
Directions:	From Route 21, just north of Naples, past the intersection of County Road 12, turn right into a large, dirt, pull-off area. N42° 37.845 - W77° 23.492
Alternative Parking:	Route 245, Hi Tor Management Area — West River Unit (boat launch). N42° 39.081 - W77° 20.426
Alternative Parking:	Sunnyside Road off Route 245, West River Fishing Access. N42° 39.378 - W77° 19.871
Alternative Parking:	Trail's endpoint at Cayward Cross Road, off Route 245. N42° 41.084 - W77° 17.382
Riding Time:	1 hour one way (If you return on roads, the round trip is 1.6 hours, and 14.6 miles round trip.)
Length:	6.8 miles one way
Difficulty:	🥾 🥾 🥾
Surface:	Mowed grass (the mowing may be sporadic, depending on current financing levels at D.E.C.)
Trail Markings:	None
Uses:	
Dogs:	OK on leash
Contact:	New York State D.E.C. 6274 Avon-Lima Road, Avon, NY 14414 (585) 226-2466 www.dec.state.ny.us

Don't let the fact that this is an old rail bed fool you into thinking it's an easy ride. As you pedal north, you don't notice a grade, but the pedaling is tough as the trail goes steadily uphill. This ride is well worth the effort, however, because you'll find scenery that you won't see on any other rail trail. You'll ride through Middlesex Valley with the towering hills of Naples on both sides.

Most of the rail bed is a raised platform through a wetland. But, because it passes through wetlands, it may be impassable in wet weather.

The Naples hills are a backdrop for the ride
on Middlesex Valley Rail Trail.

Along the way are waterfowl nesting boxes, and about one mile southwest of Cayward Cross Road is a blue heron rookery. Please be quiet, and don't disturb the birds.

The official name of this trail is the Lehigh Valley Rail Trail. But since other sections of the Lehigh are open for biking and hiking, we've called it by its historical name. The Middlesex Valley Railroad first provided service between Naples and Stanley in 1892. The line was later extended to Geneva. In 1895 the rail line was purchased by the Lehigh Valley Railroad. Service continued until 1970 when the line was abandoned due to competition from trucks and cars for the freight of coal, building materials, farm equipment, apples, grapes, beans, etc. Most of the land reverted to private ownership. This portion of the rail trail is owned by New York State as part of the Hi Tor Wildlife Management Area. It is a public hunting ground, so avoid hunting season, or at least wear blaze-orange clothing.

Trail Distance Between Major Roads:

Route 21 to Parish Hill	1.2 miles
Parish Hill to Sunnyside	2.6 miles
Sunnyside to Cayward Cross	3.0 miles

Trail Directions

- Head toward the yellow metal gate and stop sign onto a 12-foot-wide, mowed-grass path.
- Cross the first of many wooden bridges over a creek.
- Emerge from the woods to a vineyard, then a field on your right. The Naples hills tower above as a backdrop to the fields.
- Continue parallel to the creek.
- Cross the second wooden bridge. These bridges were repaired by the NY State Department of Environmental Conservation.
- Pass a yellow metal gate then cross Parish Hill Road.
- Pass another yellow metal gate and ride through a raised bed over wetlands.
- Cross the third wooden bridge. There are some short sections of ballast stone.
- Cross the forth wooden bridge, then a few more short sections of ballast.
- The trail now runs parallel to a road.
- Cross the fifth wooden bridge. You may have to walk your bike. Some of the top planks are rotted.
- Pass through a backyard of farm animals. This is home to a horse, donkey, lamb, and goat as well as many ducks, geese, guinea fowl, turkeys, chickens, and rabbits. The front of this home is a roadside farm stand which sells produce, tarts, pies, breads, snacks, and drinks.
- Pass through another yellow gate into the parking area and boat launch for Hi Tor Management Area — West River Unit.
- Head toward the first yellow gate.
- Pass more yellow gates.
- Pass the West River Fishing Access site. (The West River is on your left. Across the river is the legendary site of the first Seneca Indian village, Nundawao.)
- Cross Sunnyside Road near another West River Fishing Access site. You've ridden 3.8 miles so far.
- Pass yellow gates.
- Cross a long wooden bridge (the 6th) where the waters fork. Trailers are on the left, then a beaver dam and dens on the right.
- Cross the seventh wooden bridge. Enjoy wetlands on both sides of the path.
- Continue on a long stretch through a wooded area.
- The land again turns to wetlands, this time with clumps of wild daylilies along the shore.

- The path ends at the yellow gates at Cayward Cross Road. From here you have two options. One is to turn around and follow the rail trail back to the start. The other is to follow the roads back. The roads have good paved shoulders and are predominately downhill. Turn right (E) onto Cayward Cross Road, right onto Route 245, then right again when it ends at Route 21. This takes you back to the start. Along the way, pass an old cemetery and a roadside farm stand.

Date Enjoyed: _____

Notes:

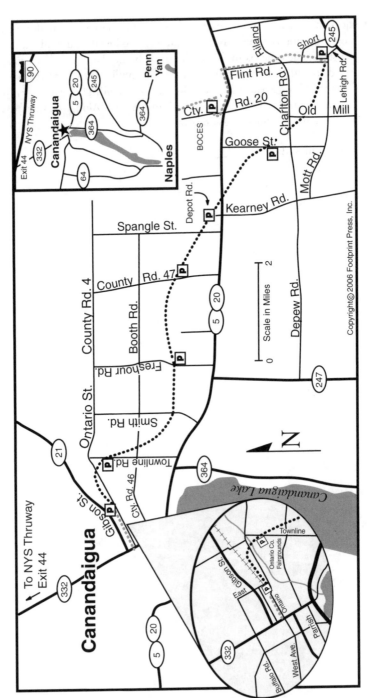

Ontario Pathways - Canandaigua to Stanley

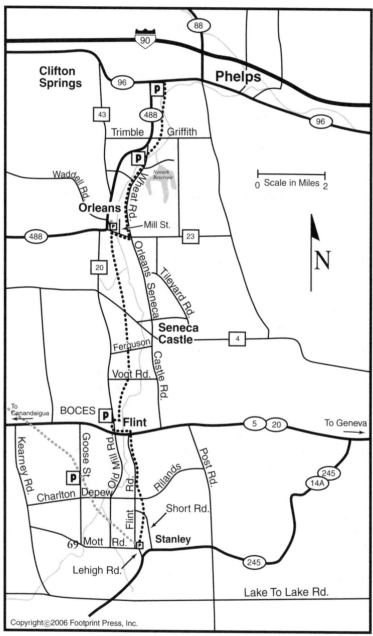

Ontario Pathways - Stanley to Phelps

11.

Ontario Pathways

Location:	Canandaigua to Stanley and Stanley to Phelps, Ontario County
Directions:	From Route 332 in downtown Canandaigua, turn left (E) onto Ontario Street just after the Ontario County Courthouse (a yellow building with a statue on its gold-domed roof). Pass the Ontario County Sheriff and Jail building. Cross active railroad tracks. The parking lot is on the left in front of an old red warehouse. N42º 53.535 - W77º 16.203

Alternative Parking: On Townline Road (County Road 10) near Ontario County Fairgrounds. N42º 53.773 - W77º 14.766

Alternative Parking: Freshour Road. N42º 51.526 - W77º 12.484

Alternative Parking: County Road 47. N42º 52.518 - W77º 10.742

Alternative Parking: Depot Road. N42º 51.759 - W77º 09.068

Alternative Parking: Goose Street. N42º 50.745 - W77º 07.555

Alternative Parking: Mott Road. N42º 49.523 - W77º 06.079

Alternative Parking: Behind the Finger Lakes Technical & Career Center (BOCES) building on County Road 20. N42º 55.108 - W77º 06.776

Alternative Parking: Off Waddell Road, at the corner of County Road 23. N42º 53.535 - W77º 16.203

Alternative Parking: Along the edge of Wheat Road (except from November through April). N42º 56.394 - W77º 05.966

Alternative Parking: On the south side of Route 96 east of the Route 488 intersection in Phelps. N42º 57.690 - W77º 05.454

Riding Time:	3.5 hours Canandaigua to Phelps
Length:	19.7 miles one way (see distances between roads below)
Difficulty:	👟 👟 (some soft grass)
Surface:	Stone dust and mowed-grass
Trail Markings:	Plastic, green-and-white signs that read "Welcome to Ontario Pathways" Green-and-yellow plastic signs that read "Warning No Motorized Vehicles, No Hunting on Trail, Ontario Pathways, Inc."

Some segments have numbered wooden posts as half-mile markers
Red metal gates at each road crossing

Uses:

Dogs: OK on leash
Contact: Ontario Pathways
P.O. Box 996, Canandaigua, NY 14424
(585) 234-7722
www.ontariopathways.org

Active railroad tracks parallel Ontario Pathways in Canandaigua.

Ontario Pathways is a grass-roots organization, formed in 1993, of people dedicated to the establishment of public-access trails throughout Ontario County. They purchased and are working to develop two rail beds abandoned by the Penn Central Corporation. Trains last thundered over this land in 1972, when Hurricane Agnes hit and damaged many of the rails. When complete, these two rail beds will cover 22 miles from Canandaigua southwest to Stanley, and from Stanley north to Phelps. Two gaps remain — both in the Stanley to Phelps leg. One requires a detour along Flint Road and Route 5 & 20 because fixing the old rail bridge over Route 5 & 20 is still on the project list. The other requires a road detour on Wheat Road in Phelps to get around some private property.

The rail bed you'll be riding started operation in 1851, as the Canandaigua Corning Line and was financed by prominent Canandaigua

Pass an old wooden water tower in Orleans, on Ontario Pathways.

residents Mark Sibley, John Granger, Oliver Phelps III, and Jared Wilson. This short line, like many of its cousins, suffered grave financial losses and changed names four times in 14 years. Even the federal government became involved when, in 1862, President Abraham Lincoln authorized the expenditure of $50,000 to revive the line so that men and supplies could be moved southward to the Civil War battlefront in Pennsylvania. Recruits rode this line to training centers in Elmira, New York, and Harrisburg, Pennsylvania.

By 1880, Canandaigua became a tourist attraction. Cargo switched from agricultural goods to passengers, as five trains ran daily between Canandaigua and Elmira. However, as with all of the railroads, business faded in the 1950s and 1960s because of competition from cars and trucks. The rail line changed hands many more times, until the merger of Northern Central with New York Central to form the Penn Central in 1968. Penn Central filed for bankruptcy in 1970, and train traffic dwindled even further. When Hurricane Agnes blew through the area in 1972, she damaged bridges, tracks, and rail beds. Penn Central abandoned the line, sold the rails for scrap, and sold the land corridor in 1994 to Ontario Pathways.

The trail is a 10-foot-wide swath through lush countryside. We rode it in the fall, pedaling over a bed of colored leaves with the canopy above blazing reds and yellows. It would be a delight to ride this trail in any season except, of course, the snow season when cross-country skis or snowshoes would be more appropriate.

Trail Distance Between Major Roads:
Canandaigua Downtown Spur

Route 332 to Ontario Street	0.4 mile
Ontario Street to East Street	0.5 mile

From 1st Parking Lot

East Street to Ontario Street	0.9 mile
Ontario Street to County Road 10 (Townline Road)	0.4 mile
County Road 10 to County Road 46	0.8 mile
County Road 46 to Smith Road	1.0 mile
Smith Road to Freshour Road	0.9 mile
Freshour Road to County Road 47	1.6 mile
County Road 47, past Spangle to Depot Road	1.7 mile
Depot Road, past Route 5&20 to Goose Street	1.8 mile
Goose Street to Depew/Charlton Road	0.4 mile
Depew/Charlton Road to Old Mill Road	0.5 mile
Old Mill Road to Mott Road	0.7 mile

Stanley

Mott Road to Short Road	0.6 mile
Short Road to Rilands Road	0.3 mile
Rilands Road to end of trail at Flint Road	0.2 mile
Road segment (Flint Road to County Road 20)	0.8 mile

BOCES on County Road 20 to Vogt Road	0.7 mile
Vogt Road to Ferguson Road	0.4 mile
Ferguson Road to County Road 4	0.5 mile
County Road 4 to County Road 23	1.3 mile
Road segment (Waddell Road to Wheat Road)	2.2 miles
Wheat Road to Trimble Griffith Road	0.5 mile
Trimble Griffith Road to Route 96	1.2 miles

Phelps

Trail Directions (Canandaigua to Phelps)
From Canandaigua:

- From the parking area on Ontario Street head northeast on the trail, away from the city of Canandaigua, parallel to an active set of railroad tracks. If you're lucky, a train will come by.
- Cross East Street.
- Pass a red metal gate. On the left, watch for the cement pillar with "S73" denoting 73 miles to Syracuse.
- After a while, the trail and railroad tracks diverge.
- Head downhill past a red gate. Cross Ontario Street.
- Head uphill, then cross a long wooden bridge over Canandaigua Outlet.
- The Ontario County Fair Grounds appear on your right.
- Cross Townline Road (County Road 10) near the entrance to the Fair Grounds.
- Cross County Road 46. You've now come 2.4 miles.
- Cross a dirt driveway.
- Cross Smith Road. Then cross several farm lanes.
- Pass a red metal gate, then a farm lane.
- Pass another farm lane, buildings, and a sheep pasture on the left. Continue straight on the trail, passing a farm pond and a farm lane to the right.
- At 5.9 miles, cross County Road 47. Pass a metal gate.
- Cross several farm lanes.
- Pass a red metal gate, cross Spangle Road, then pass another gate.
- Bear right heading downhill. Cross a farm lane that goes past old railroad abutments, then head uphill back to the railroad bed.
- You'll see houses on the right and the end of Depot Road where parking is available. You've come 7.6 miles.
- Cross a farm lane, then pass a metal gate.
- Cross over Routes 5 & 20 on a railroad bridge.
- The trail dips at a farm lane then crosses a small bridge.
- Cross more farm lanes.
- Pass a metal gate just before crossing Goose Street at 9.4 miles.

In Fall, the Ontario Pathways tunnel is ablaze in vivid colors.

- Cross Depew/Charlton Road.
- Cross a long bridge.
- Cross Old Mill Road at 10.3 miles.
- Cross Flint Road.
- Soon, reach the gravel parking area tucked between Mott and Lehigh Roads.

From Stanley:
- Take an immediate left before the parking area, heading north.
- Cross Short Road, then Rilands Road.
- The trail will stop on Flint Road.

- Turn right, and head north on Flint Road.
- Pass the Seneca Town Hall (restrooms).
- At Routes 5 & 20 turn left and dip under the old rail road bridge.
- Take the first right onto County Road 20.
- Ride north on County Road 20, then turn right before the large red and white sign "Finger Lakes Technical & Career Center."
- Ride to the back of the parking area and up the grass hill behind the buildings.
- Bear right, passing a trail to the left. Meet the Ontario Pathways Trail and turn left. (To the right is the old railroad bridge over Routes 5 & 20.)
- Cross 2 small bridges then pass a gate.
- Cross ATV paths and reach Vogt Road at 13.6 miles.
- Cross Ferguson Road, then in another 0.5 mile, cross County Road 4.
- Ride over a creek on an earthen embankment.
- Cross over a pipeline.
- Flint Creek comes and goes from view far below. In spots you'll ride close to a precipitous ledge.
- Reach County Road 23 at 15.8 miles. (A large parking area and a wood-shingled water tower are at this corner.)
- Turn right on County Road 23 to begin the 2.2-mile road section. Cross Flint Creek and pass Mill Street.
- Turn left onto Wheat Road, heading north.
- Pass roads to the left then right.
- Cross Flint Creek.
- Turn right to pick up the Ontario Pathways Trail (just south of the Route 488 junction).
- Cross Griffith Road.
- Cross a small wooden bridge.
- Cross Flint Creek. Notice the waterfalls to your right.
- Pass old railroad bridge abutments.
- Rest at the bench.
- Cross Flint Creek again.
- Reach the Route 96 parking area.

Date Enjoyed: _____

Notes:

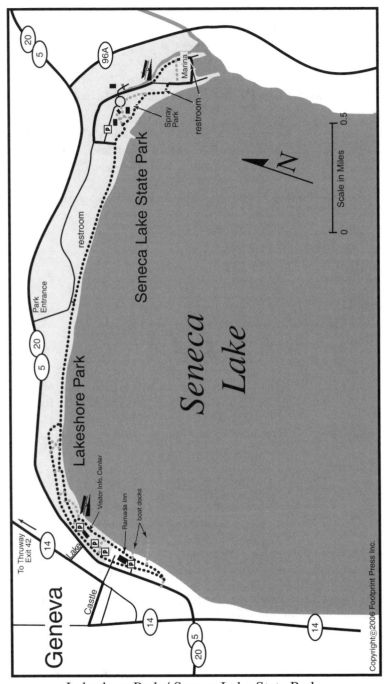

Lakeshore Park / Seneca Lake State Park

12.

Lakeshore Park / Seneca Lake State Park

Location: North end of Seneca Lake in Geneva, Ontario County
Directions: From Route 5 & 20, turn east on Lake Street, into the visitor center parking lot in Lakeshore Park.
N42° 52.516 - W76° 57.810
Alternative Parking: Parking is available in Seneca Lake State Park. (There is a $6 per vehicle entrance fee.)
N42° 52.434 - W76° 56.743
Riding Time: 1 hour loop
Length: 9-mile loop
Difficulty:
Surface: Paved, minor gravel section
Trail Markings: ½-mile markings along the Lakeshore Trail
Uses:

Dogs: OK on leash
Facilities: Several restrooms are available in Seneca Lake State Park. There is an ice cream stand south of the Ramada Inn and a snack bar in the visitor center.
Admission: Free via Lakeshore Park, $6/vehicle via Seneca Lake State Park
Contacts: Seneca Lake State Park
1 Lakefront Drive, Geneva, NY 14456
(315) 789-2331

Geneva Area Chamber of Commerce
35 Lakefront Drive, P.O. Box 587
Geneva, NY 14456
(315) 789-1776 www.genevany.com

Seneca Lake is named after the Seneca Indian Nation, one of the Six Nations of the Iroquois Confederacy. The Senecas inhabited these shores long before white settlers arrived.

Seneca Lake is 36 miles long and 632 feet deep at its deepest spot, which makes it the deepest and second longest of the eleven Finger Lakes (Cayuga Lake is 38 miles long). Holding more than four trillion gallons of water, Seneca Lake is the largest Finger Lake. Because of its volume, Seneca Lake rarely freezes in winter. The water moderates the temperature of the surrounding land and makes the area prime for vineyards and orchards.

Seneca Lake State Park was brush, trees, and marsh until 1922, when the city of Geneva developed it into a park. Title was passed to New York State in 1957.

The route described incorporates the paths through Lakeshore Park and Seneca Lake State Park. You'll ride along the lakeshore, shaded by large willow trees. Bring picnic food, there's plenty of picnic tables and grills to enjoy a lake-side meal. Most of the route is paved, but sections in Seneca Lake State Park are somewhat rough for in-line skating. This is an active trail, popular with walkers, dog walkers and bicyclists.

Trail Directions
- From the Lakeshore Park parking lot head west along the paved trail beside Route 5 and 20, heading back toward Geneva.
- Cross Lake Street at the entrance to the park.
- Cross Castle Street.
- Ride in front of Ramada Inn.
- Cross the entrance to Ramada Inn. Pass an ice cream stand.
- At the next intersection, turn left and follow the brick path along the lakeshore. (The trail to the right goes through a tunnel and dead-ends.The trail straight ahead is also a dead-end.)
- Pass a small gravel segment.
- Ride behind Ramada Inn.
- Continue close to the water.
- Ride behind the visitor center. It has a snack bar.
- Pass a boat ramp as you cut through the Lakeshore Park parking lot.
- At the far end of the parking lot, cut over to the bike path. This is the original Route 5 and 20 which often got washed out from high water in Seneca Lake.
- At the next several intersections, continue straight to stay near the water.
- Pass a barrier into Seneca Lake State Park.
- Continue along the lake, passing three park buildings and a spray park.
- Continue along the lake as the trail turns to gravel. When it ends cross the short grass segment to the park road.
- Turn right onto the park road . At the marina circle turn left.
- At the next marina circle, turn left and follow a gravel road, past a boat launch, back to the park road.

Ride the north shore of Seneca Lake.

- Turn right and follow the park road. Pass the park buildings and a large parking lot, then turn left on a connector road to return to the lakeshore bike path.
- Turn right onto the lakeshore bike path.
- Pass the barrier.
- Turn right at the first intersection.
- Bear right past several intersecting trails until you reach the Lakeshore Park parking lot.

Date Enjoyed: _____

Notes:

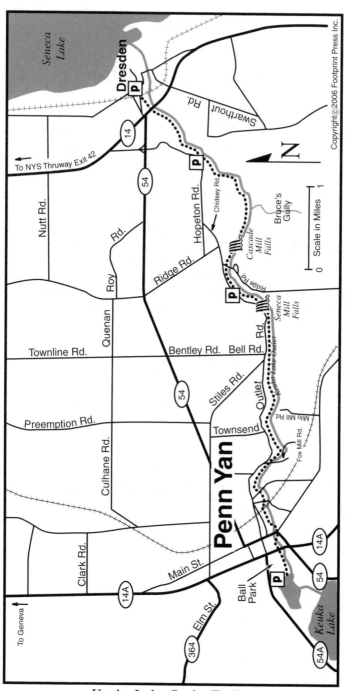

Keuka Lake Outlet Trail

13.

Keuka Lake Outlet Trail

Location:	Dresden to Penn Yan, Yates County
Directions:	From Route 14 south along the west side of Seneca Lake, turn left (E) at Route 54 heading toward Main Street, Dresden. There is a Citgo gas station and the Crossroads Ice Cream Shop at the corner. At the Crossroads Ice Cream Shop, take an immediate right onto Seneca Street. Parking is on your right just before the railroad tracks. N42° 40.861 - W76° 57.520

Alternative Parking: Penn Yan, Marsh Development Project, Little League Baseball, on Route 54A (Elm Street). N42° 39.513 - W77° 3.632

Alternative Parking: Outlet Road. N42° 39.918 - W77° 0.078

Alternative Parking: Hopeton Road. N42° 40.291 - W76° 58.280

Riding Time: 1 hour one way

Length: 6.8 miles one way

Trail Distance Between Parking Areas:

Dresden to Hopeton Road	1.0 mile
Hopeton Road to Outlet Road	2.0 miles
Outlet Road to Route 54A	3.8 miles

Difficulty:

Surface: Dirt (western end is paved)

Trail Markings: Green and white metal "Trail" signs

Uses:

Dogs: OK on leash

Contact: Friends of the Outlet
P.O. Box 65, Dresden, NY 14441
www.keukaoutlettrail.net

The strip of land you will be riding from Seneca Lake to Keuka Lake is steeped in history. You'll see evidence of places and events from several bygone eras as you ride westward.

In the middle of the nineteenth century, two fingers of water connected the 274-foot drop between Keuka and Seneca Lakes, the outlet to power

Rest a while and enjoy Seneca Mill Falls.

mills, and the Crooked Lake Canal for boat traffic. A dam and guardhouse in Penn Yan controlled the water flow to both. The outlet, which still carries water from one lake to the next, was formed by a ground fault in the Tully limestone allowing water to run between the two lakes. Along its banks, you'll see remnants of the many mills which once harnessed the water power.

The first white settlers arrived in this area around 1788, attracted by the reliable water source at the outlet. In 1789 Seneca Mill was built along the raging waters of Keuka Lake Outlet to grind flour with a 26-foot, overshot flywheel. From then until 1827, a small religious group called the Society of Universal Friends built 12 dams and many mills that helped make the area a thriving community. The mills and shops produced flour (gristmills), lumber (sawmills), tool handles, linseed oil, plaster, and liquor (distilleries). There were two triphammer forges, eight fulling and carding mills, tanneries, and weavers making cotton and wool cloth. By 1835, 30 to 40 mills were in operation. But, by 1900, only five mills remained, mainly making paper from straw. The last water-turbine mill ceased operation in 1968.

In 1833 New York State opened the Crooked Lake Canal to span the six miles between the two lakes and move farm products to eastern markets. The canal was four feet deep and had 28 wooden locks. It took a vessel six hours to journey through the canal. As business boomed in the mills, the state widened and deepened the canal and replaced the wooden locks with stone. But the canal lost money every year of its 44-year history, so in 1877 the state auctioned off all the machinery and stone. Only the towpath remained. In 1844 a railroad was built on the towpath. Initially operated by the Penn Yan and New York Railway Company, it eventually became part of the New York Central System. Railway men called it the "Corkscrew Railway" because of its countless twists and turns. The line operated until 1972 when the tracks were washed out by the flood from Hurricane Agnes.

A local group interested in recreational use of the ravine convinced the town of Penn Yan to buy the property in 1981. Since then, it has been developed and maintained by a volunteer group called the Friends of the Outlet. Trail signs and outhouses were added along the route.

Reference Guides: Purchase an illustrated guide to the Keuka Lake Outlet for $1.00 from the Yates County Historian, 110 Court Street, Penn Yan, NY 14527. A packet of information on the history of the mill sites, canal, and railroad of the Keuka Lake Outlet is available for $3.00 at stores in Penn Yan.

Trail Directions
- The trail leads downhill from the back-right corner of the Dresden parking lot, heading west.
- Cross under the Route 14 bridge. The land you're on used to be the Dresden Mill Pond.
- The wetland to your right (north of the trail) is the old Crooked Lake Canal.
- Cross two wooden bridges.
- Notice the steep cliffs on both sides. Where the canal and outlet are close together was the location of Lock 3. Watch for the cement and rebar millstone.
- Cross a dirt road. This was Hopeton Road, which in the 1790s connected Geneva to Bath through the town of Hopeton. To your left you can still see remnants of the iron-pony, truss bridge over the outlet. The bridge was built in 1840 and rests on stone abutments. This area was once a community of mills. Hopeton Grist Mill was located just beyond the dirt road on the left. Nothing remains of it today.
- On your left is a pleasant rest area with large rocks where you can sit along the water.
- Across the outlet, Bruces Gully cascades water over three waterfalls to join the outlet. Eventually the Friends of the Outlet plan to build a hiking trail through the gully. The dark gray rock, which peels in thin layers, is Genesee shale.

84

Remains of a papermill from 1890.

•Pass a cement pillar on your right. The big "W" on the pillar signaled the train conductor to blow his whistle.

- At the two-mile point are the remains of the J.T. Baker Chemical Company, manufacturers of the pesticide carbine bisulfide until 1968. At one time, this was also the site of a gristmill and several paper mills.
- Here you'll see your first waterfall. The top step of the falls was the old dam, constructed in 1827 and the last of the 12 dams built along the outlet. Both Cascade Mill and Mallory's Mill used the water that was held back by this dam.
- Follow the wide gravel path through the building area.
- Pass old Kelly Tire buildings. The Friends of the Outlet renovated these buildings into the Alfred Jensen Memorial Visitor Center. It's a good place to stop if you need a restroom.
- Follow the green and white trail signs as the trail branches to the left.
- At 2.6 miles, cross the paved Ridge Road. In 1805 May's Mills stood at this site. It had a gristmill, a sawmill, and a post office. In the 1820s this area was home to a cotton factory, then a distillery.
- Continue along the outlet. Outlet Road parallels close to the trail.
- Just over a culvert is another cement post displaying a "W," then another cement marker with "D3" which told the conductor that Dresden was three miles away. This means that you're almost halfway to Penn Yan.
- Pass a parking lot off Outlet Road. The brick remnants on the right were once a factory that turned rags into paper.
- Look for the large rock between the trail and the outlet. A plaque on the side facing the outlet commemorates John Sheridan, a lawyer who negotiated the purchase of land for the Keuka Lake Outlet Preservation Area. The stone remnants across the outlet were once a forge. At one time a road crossed over the dam at this spot. Seneca Mill, the first mill site, was located at this falls, the largest falls on the outlet.
- On your right (away from the outlet) is a stone wall with a large round opening. This used to house a pipe to vent train smoke out of the valley.
- The machinery that remains at the top of the dam controlled water flow through a sluiceway. The original Friends Mill, a complex of paper and gristmills, was here. There's now a nice picnic pavilion here.
- The trail bears right through Lock 17, which was the downstream end of a series of four locks needed to maneuver the elevation drop.
- You're now biking in a ravine of the old canal bed. In May this segment of trail is lined with trillium. It's also an active beaver area.
- Pass another cement whistle sign on the right.
- The cement wall in the water is the end of a race from Milo Mills. The stagnant water on the left is the raceway. From here to Penn Yan was the most industrialized section of the outlet.

- A large brick chimney towers over the remains of a paper mill, built in 1890, burned in 1910, and then rebuilt. You can still see the 17-foot flywheel which used two miles of hemp cable and was run by a steam engine. The machinery was manufactured at the Rochester foundry at Brown's Race.
- At 4.4 miles, cross Milo Mill Road.
- Cross a bridge over a wood-lined sluice. This used to carry water to Shutt's Mill, which dates back to about 1850.
- A small side path immediately to the left leads to the ruins of Shutt's Mill. You can still see the stone vats from this paper mill which manufactured wallboard. Shutt's Mill burned in 1933. The first mill at this site was a sawmill built in 1812. It was followed by a wool mill, a gristmill, and a fulling mill. Beware of the poison ivy in the area.
- The waterfall on the far side of the outlet, just before a road and bridge, is outflow from the municipal sewage plant.
- Cross a road. Dibbles Mill used to make wooden wheels in this area.
- The green shed across the road on the right was a blacksmith shop from canal times (around 1838). The blacksmith specialized in shoeing mules.
- At 5.5 miles, cross paved Fox Mill Road. If you take a left on Fox Mill Road, then a quick right toward the outlet, you'll find remains from the Fox Mill, which manufactured straw paper. The stone for the walls was moved here from the dismantled locks of Crooked Lake Canal around 1865.
- Pass a sign for St. John's Mill. Other than the sign, there's nothing to see. The mill used to be across the outlet.
- Cross paved Cherry Street. The trail becomes paved.
- Pass under a railroad trestle called "High Bridge." It was originally built of wood in 1850 and was rebuilt in 1890.
- The large circular hollow just after the trestle was once a turntable for the train.
- Pass signs for an exercise trail. After the chin-up bars on the right, a small path leads left to another cement railroad marker "D6," indicating six miles from Dresden.
- Reach the wooden bridge which served as a railroad trestle to Birkett Mills in 1824. Birkett Mills took their water turbines out in 1947.
- At 6.5 miles, pass under the Main Street (Penn Yan) bridge which was built in 1884 from canal stone. This area used to have the guardhouse for the canal. The dam on the right is used to control water level in Keuka Lake. The brown building you can see was a grain warehouse. At one time this section of trail was home to several woodworking factories, a cooperage, and a sash-and-blind factory.
- Pass through a park, then cross the pedestrian bridge over the outlet.

- Continue through Penn Yan Recreation Complex on the paved path. You pass restrooms, a boat launch, tennis courts, and a small playground.
- Cross another wooden bridge over Sucker Brook.
- Pass through the athletic fields to the parking lot in Marsh Development Project on Route 54A.

Date Enjoyed: _____

Notes:

Rides in Seneca, Schuyler & Tompkins Counties

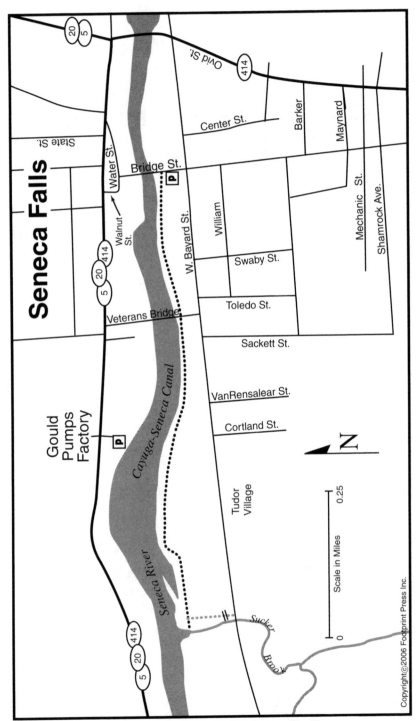

Frank J. Ludovico Sculpture Trail

14.

Frank J. Ludovico Sculpture Trail

Location: Seneca Falls, Seneca County

Directions: Follow Route 414 south in Seneca Falls. Over the canal, turn right (W) on West Bayard Street, then right (N) on Bridge Street. Park in front of the stores on Bridge Street, south of the canal bridge. (The Bridge Street bridge over the canal is labeled Clarence Street on the bridge.)   N42° 54.555 - W76° 48.051

Alternative Parking: A public parking area south of Route 5 & 20, across from the Gould Pumps factory.
N42° 54.618 - W76° 48.603

Riding Time: 15 minutes round trip

Length: 1.7 mile round trip

Difficulty: 🥾🥾

Surface: Stone dust for the first 1.1 mile, then dirt double-track

Trail Markings: None

Uses: 🚶 🚴 🎿 🏃 ♿

Dogs: OK on leash

Contact: Ludovico Sculpture Trail's Visitors and Arts Center
61 Ovid St. (Route 414), P.O. Box 0566
Seneca Falls, NY 13148

Friends of the Frank Ludovico Sculpture Trail
60 Cayuga Street, Seneca Falls, NY 13148
(315) 568-8204

The Frank J. Ludovico Sculpture Trail is a trail that parallels the south shore of the Erie Canal in Seneca Falls. It will eventually be part of the Erie Canalway Trail that reaches across New York State.

This trail is special in that it's a sculpture garden as well as a trail. The first sculpture that was installed along the trail is called, "The Status of Women" and commemorates six important points in women's history. You'll also find statues of Amelia Bloomer and Mary Baker Eddy, two prominent women in women's suffrage.

One of the sculptures along the Sculpture Trail.

2003 saw the unveiling of a sculpture titled "The Bacchus" by artist Hyon Telarico. The metal sculpture was named after a Roman wine God and stands nearly 30 feet tall. In 2005, two additional sculptures were installed, featuring Irish and Italian canal diggers. Irish and Italian immigrants figured prominently in the building of the canal. The concrete figures honoring that effort were created by Brian Pfeiffer of Bennington in Wyoming County. Trail Director Wilhelmina Pusmucans said that after reading about Pfeiffer in a Buffalo newspaper, she called him and he agreed to produce the sculptures free of charge. Historian David Hanna was consulted for accuracy of the period clothing worn by the Irish construction workers of the 1820s and the turn-of-the-century Italian workers. Additional sculptures are planned for the future.

Wilhelmina Pusmucans is the founder of a Friends of the Trail group that works to build and maintain the trail and to add sculptures. The group sells commemorative bricks for $50 each that get installed around the base of the various sculptures along the trail. For more information, use the contact information listed above.

In addition to the sculptures to view, this rail-trail offers splendid views of the Erie Canal. The first 1.1 mile is an easy ride on a stone dust trail.

The remaining milage is currently a dirt double-track, but it's still an easy ride.

Trail Directions
- From Bridge Street head west on the trail, passing the sculptures.
- Continue straight when the trail turns to dirt.
- When the trail dead-ends at Sucker Brook, turn around and head back to Bridge Street.

Date Enjoyed: _____

Notes:

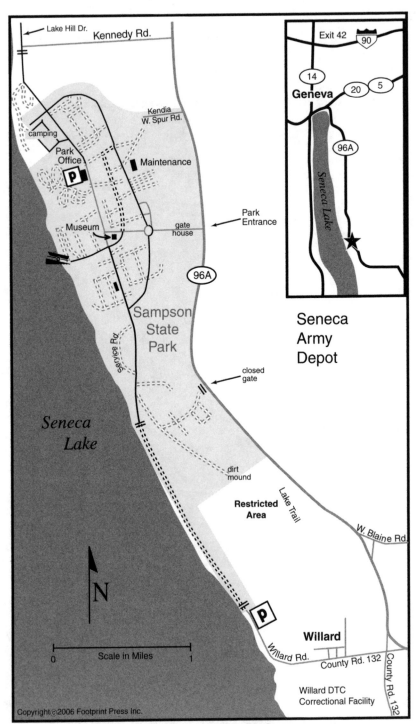

Sampson State Park

15.

Sampson State Park – Lake Trail

Location:	On the east side of Seneca Lake, Seneca County
Directions:	Take Route 96A south from Geneva. Pass Sampson State Park. Where Route 96A bends east, bear right on County Road 132. Turn west on Willard Road. Follow Willard Road as it bends right and parallels the shore of Seneca Lake. The parking area is on the right of Willard Road at the barrier. N42º 41.243 - W76º 53.058
Alternative Parking:	In Sampson State Park (Costs $6 per vehicle from Memorial Day to Labor Day.) N42º 44.056 - W76º 54.600
Riding Time:	1.2 hour loop
Length:	7.8-mile loop
Difficulty:	
Surface:	Stone dust trail and old paved roads
Trail Markings:	None
Uses:	
Dogs:	OK on leash
Admission:	Free from Willard entrance, $6 through the park
Contact:	Sampson State Park 6096 Route 96A, Romulus, NY 14541 (315) 585-6392

This is a family biking paradise. A network of abandoned roads from the Sampson Naval Training Station provide hours of nooks and crannies to explore. The trails (roads) are paved, but the abandoned ones are being overgrown with weeds and undermined with roots. This combination keeps cars out and means safe bicycling.

The first humans to use this area were nomadic hunters. By the early 1600s, the Seneca Indians had established an agricultural community called Kendaia. This settlement was burned by the Continental Army during the Revolutionary War. After the war, much of the land between Seneca and Cayuga Lakes was awarded to soldiers as payment for their

The Lake Trail parallels Seneca Lake.

service. They moved in and established farms where the Indians once thrived.

A century and a half later, with the outbreak of World War II, quiet farm life made way for the second largest navel training station in the country. It was named for a Palmyra resident, Rear Admiral William T. Sampson. After the war, Sampson State College was located on the base to educate returning servicemen. Sampson was used as an air force base during the Korean War, and became a state park in 1960.

The old drill fields and other cleared lands are slowing growing up in grasses, wildflowers, shrubs, and trees. Some buildings have been removed, but others remain as shells of their former selves. Use your imagination as you ride through this area to conjure up images of the days when the naval base thrived.

Your ride will begin on the Lake Trail, a road of many names. It began as a Seneca Indian trail. While used as a World War II Naval station it was called Mahan Road. This name was changed to Liberator Road when the Air Force managed the area as a training facility. Maps today label it as East Lake Road, but it is closed to cars. Lake Trail was resurfaced in 1997. It runs for 1.7 miles from the parking area on Willard Road to Sampson State Park.

Once in the park, your ride will loop around some rarely used back roads at the north end. Finish with a ride back down the Lake Trail.

Along Lake Trail you'll find numbered wooden posts that identify trees. In 1998 Boy Scout Jonathan Lanning installed these as his Eagle project. His brochure, which gives the scientific names, descriptions, and uses of each of the following types of trees, is available at the Sampson State Park Office and Recreation Building.

1. Northern White Cedar
2. Eastern Red Cedar
3. Eastern Cottonwood
4. Sugar Maple
5. Basswood
6. Black Locust
7. White Oak
8. Big-toothed Aspen
9. Black Walnut
10. Shagbark Hickory
11. White Ash
12. Red Oak
13. Hop Hornbeam

If you head south to the trailhead in Willard, you'll pass Sampson State Park on the right and the fenced area of Seneca Army Depot on the left. Watch carefully along the way. The deer herd in Seneca Army Depot includes rare white deer (not technically albino deer). As we drove south, once, we spotted 3 deer just inside the fence. One was a normal brown white-tailed deer, one was a grazing white doe, and on the ground rested a white buck with full antlers.

Trail Directions
•From the Willard Road parking area, head north past large boulders, heading uphill on Lake Trail.

- Pass several trails and old roads intersecting Lake Trail.
- At 0.9 mile, a gravel trail on the left leads down to the shore of Seneca Lake.
- More old roads intersect, but continue straight.
- At 1.7 miles pass a gate.
- Continue straight on the paved road. Two major roads on the right lead to dead-ends.
- Pass a service road and a maintenance building.
- At 3.1 miles you'll reach a major road intersection. The large, fenced-in, red brick Navy Museum building will be kitty-corner to the right. (To the left is the boat launch.) Turn right.
- Cross the main entrance road.
- Continue straight, past road intersections and a log over the road, until the road ends at a "T." Turn right (E).
- At the next intersection turn right (S), and pass a block building on the left.
- Continue straight. At a "Y" bear right.
- At 4.8 miles, reach the traffic circle with a memorial statue. Bear left around the circle to continue straight across.
- Pass more roads. At a "T," turn left (S).
- Continue south and follow Lake Trail downhill to the parking area.

Date Enjoyed: _____

Notes:

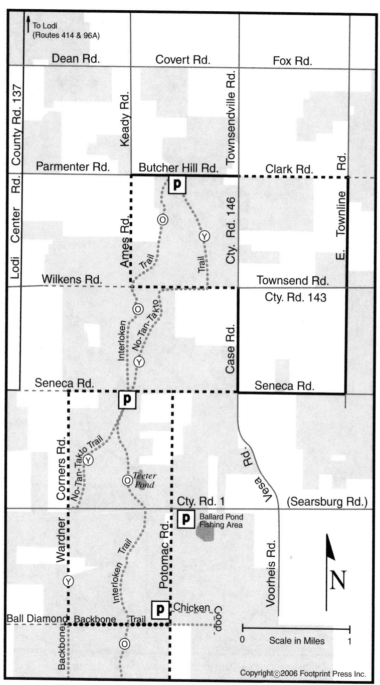

To Lodi
(Routes 414 & 96A)

Dean Rd.

Covert Rd.

Fox Rd.

County Rd. 137

Keady Rd.

Townsendville Rd.

Parmenter Rd.

Butcher Hill Rd.

Clark Rd.

Lodi Center Rd.

Rd.

P

Cty. Rd. 146

Ames Rd.

Ⓞ

Ⓨ

Trail

Trail

E. Townline

Wilkens Rd.

Townsend Rd.

Cty. Rd. 143

Ⓞ

No-Tan-Takto

Interloken

Case Rd.

Ⓨ

Seneca Rd.

Seneca Rd.

P

Corners Rd.

No-Tan-Takto Trail

Ⓨ

Vesa

Rd.

(Searsburg Rd.)

Ⓞ

Teeter
Pond

Cty. Rd. 1

P

Ballard Pond
Fishing Area

Wardner

Interloken Trail

Potomac Rd.

Voorheis Rd.

N

Ⓨ

P

Chicken

Coop

Ball Diamond

Backbone Trail

Backbone

Ⓞ

0   Scale in Miles   1

Copyright © 2006 Footprint Press Inc.

Finger Lakes National Forest (North Section)

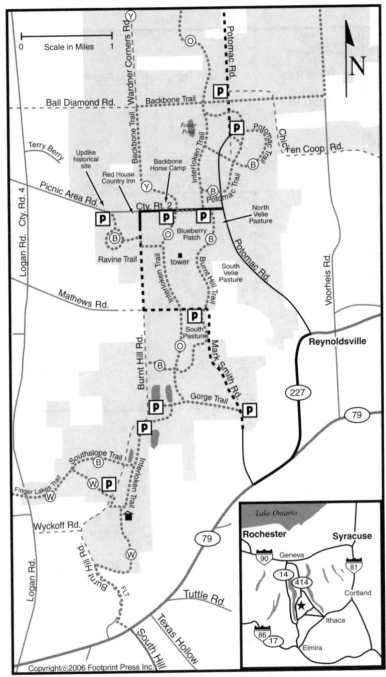

Finger Lakes National Forest (South Section)

16.

Finger Lakes National Forest

Location: Between Seneca and Cayuga Lakes, Schuyler County
Directions: Take Route 96A south along the eastern side of Seneca Lake, through Ovid and Lodi. Just past Lodi, turn south onto Lodi Center Road (County Road 137). Take the third left (E) onto Parmenter Road. When it becomes Butcher Hill Road, the Interloken Trail parking lot will be on the right.   N42° 54.555 - W76° 48.051
Alternative Parking: Trails junction on Seneca Road.
N42° 32.627 - W76° 47.976
Alternative Parking: Ballard Pond parking area on County Road 1.
N42° 31.704 - W76° 47.248
Alternative Parking: Parking at corner of Potomac Road & Backbone Trail.   N42° 30.249 - W76° 47.406
Alternative Parking: Potomac Campground parking on Potomac Road.
N42° 29.719 - W76° 47.295
Alternative Parking: North Velie Pasture parking Area on County Road 2.   N42° 29.040 - W76° 47.678
Alternative Parking: South Pasture parking on Mathews Road.
N42° 28.172 - W76° 47.666
Alternative Parking: Gorge Trail parking on Mark Smith Road.
N42° 27.267 - W76° 47.160
Surface: Mostly packed dirt roads, some paved roads
Trail Markings: Street signs (sometimes)
Uses:

Dogs: OK on leash
Contact: Finger Lakes National Forest
5218 State Road 414, Hector, NY 14841-9707
(607) 546-4470

The Finger Lakes National Forest encompasses 16,000 acres of land and has over 30 miles of interconnecting hiking trails. The trails are not open to bicycles. The forest is, however, crisscrossed by a network of single-lane dirt roads that are excellent for biking. These roads are open April 1 through November 30 only. Because the national forest is open to hunting, biking during hunting season is not recommended.

From a bicycle you can explore the deep forests and steep hills of this varied countryside. The forest contains a five-acre blueberry patch. What better treat on any bike excursion than devouring a handful of freshly picked blueberries. August and September are the best months to find ripe blueberries. This forest also offers overnight camping and has a privately owned bed-and-breakfast (Red House Country Inn B&B, Picnic Area Road, (607) 546-8566), making it a perfect weekend getaway. Contact the Finger Lakes National Forest for additional information on camping. Two hiking loops are described in the book *Take A Hike — Family Walks in New York's Finger Lakes Region.*

The area around the Finger Lakes National Forest was originally inhabited by the Iroquois Indians, though little is known of their use of the region. In 1790, the area was divided into 600-acre military lots and distributed among Revolutionary War veterans as payment for their service. These early settlers cleared the land for production of hay and small grains, such as buckwheat. As New York City grew, a strong market for these products developed, encouraging more intensive agriculture. The farmers prospered until the middle of the nineteenth century, when a series of unfortunate events occurred: the popularity of motorized transportation in urban centers (reducing the number of horses to be fed), gradual depletion of the soil resource, and competition from midwestern agriculture.

Between 1890 and the Great Depression, over a million acres of farmland were abandoned in south-central New York State. In the 1930s, it was obvious that farmers in many parts of the country could no longer make a living from their exhausted land. Environmental damage worsened as they cultivated the land more and more intensively to make ends meet. Several pieces of legislation were passed, including the Emergency Relief Act of 1933 and the Bankhead-Jones Farm Tenant Act of 1937, to address these problems. A new government agency, the Resettlement Administration, was formed to carry out the new laws. This agency not only directed the relocation of farmers to better land or other jobs, but also directed the purchase of marginal farmland by the federal government.

Between 1938 and 1941, more than 100 farms were purchased in the Finger Lakes National Forest area and administered by the Soil Conservation Service. Because this was done on a willing-seller, willing-buyer basis, the resulting federal ownership resembled a patchwork quilt. The land was named the Hector Land Use Area and was managed to stabilize the soil by planting conifers and developing a grazing program. Individual livestock owners were allowed to graze animals on the pasture land to show how less intensive agriculture could still make productive use of the land.

By the 1950s, many of the objectives of the Hector Land Use Area had been met, and the public was becoming interested in the concept of multiple uses of public land. In 1954, administration responsibilities were transferred to the U.S. Forest Service. In 1985, the name was changed to the Hector Ranger District, Finger Lakes National Forest.

Today, this national forest is used for recreation, hunting, forestry, grazing of private livestock, preservation of wildlife habitat, education, and research. It is a treasure available for all of us to enjoy.

Short Loop Option

Riding Time: 1.2 hour loop
Length: 7.8-mile loop
Difficulty: 👣 👣 👣

Trail Directions

- From the Interloken Trail parking lot, head east on Parmenter/ Butcher Hill Road. In 0.6 mile, pass Case Road/County Road 146. Continue straight, heading downhill for 1.0 mile on the dirt road, which changes its name to Butcher Hill/Clark Road.
- At East Townline Road turn right (S) onto this dirt road. It is paved in front of houses.
- Pass County Road 143, then turn right (W) onto Seneca Road.
- Turn right onto Case Road/County Road 146.
- In 0.9 mile, turn left onto Townsend Road/County Road 143.
- Take the first right (N) onto Ames Road, which is a narrow dirt road. Pass Interloken Trail.
- Turn right and head east on Parmenter/Butcher Hill Road. The parking lot is on your right in 0.3 mile.

Date Enjoyed: _____

Notes:

Medium Loop Option

Riding Time: 2 hour loop
Length: 12.7-mile loop
Difficulty:

Trail Directions

- From the Interloken Trail parking lot, head east on Parmenter/ Butcher Hill Road. In 0.6 mile, pass Case Road/County Road 146. Continue straight, heading downhill for 1.0 mile on the dirt road, which changes its name to Butcher Hill/Clark Road.
- At East Townline Road turn right (S) onto this dirt road. It is paved in front of houses.
- Pass County Road 143, then turn right (W) onto Seneca Road.
- Follow Seneca Road for 1.0 mile passing Vesa Road and County Road 146/Case Road. At the stop sign, turn left (S) onto Potomac Road. This is a dirt road with rolling hills.
- After 1.0 mile, there is a stop sign and a Ballard Pasture sign as you approach paved County Road 1. Continue straight (S).
- Pass a "Horse Crossing" sign. The terrain levels out. Two miles from County Road 1 is a parking lot on the right (W) for the Backbone Trail and Foster Pond. Chicken Coop Road heads to the east.
- Turn right and follow Backbone Trail/Ball Diamond Road west. Pass Interloken Trail.
- Turn right onto Wardner Corners Road. Pass County Road 1.
- At the end, turn right onto Seneca Road.
- Pass Potomac Road, then take the next left onto Case Road/County Road 146.
- In 0.9 mile, turn left onto Townsend Road/County Road 143. Only 2.2 more miles, and you're done.
- Take the first right (N) onto Ames Road, which is a narrow dirt road. Pass Interloken Trail.
- Turn right and head east on Parmenter/Butcher Hill Road. The parking lot is on your right in 0.3 mile.

Date Enjoyed: _____

Notes:

Long, Hilly Loop Option

Riding Time: 4 hour loop
Length: 25.1-mile loop
Difficulty: 👣 👣 👣 👣

Trail Directions

- From the Interloken Trail parking lot, head east on Parmenter/Butcher Hill Road. In 0.6 mile, pass Case Road/County Road 146. Continue straight, heading downhill for 1.0 mile on the dirt road, which changed its name to Butcher Hill/Clark Road.
- At East Townline Road turn right (S) onto this dirt road. It is paved in front of houses.
- Pass County Road 143, then turn right (W) onto Seneca Road.
- Follow Seneca Road for 1.0 mile passing Vesa Road and County Road 146/Case Road. At the stop sign, turn left (S) onto Potomac Road. This is a dirt road with rolling hills.
- After 1.0 mile, there is a stop sign and a Ballard Pasture sign as you approach paved County Road 1. Continue straight (S).
- Pass a "Horse Crossing" sign. The terrain levels out. Two miles from County Road 1 is a parking lot for the Backbone Trail and Foster Pond. Chicken Coop Road heads to the east. Continue straight.
- Pass the parking lot for Potomac Group Campground. The dirt road curves southwest and heads downhill.
- Continue south past Picnic Area Road and another parking area.
- Pass a national forest sign, cross a small creek, and pass a few houses. Potomac Road ends at paved Route 227. You've come 9.4 miles so far.
- Turn right (SW) onto Route 227. Head downhill past a gravel pit and the Hector Town Hall. Continue on Route 227 for 2.8 miles.
- Turn right (W) onto paved Route 79. Travel 0.4 mile more and you are back to dirt roads.
- At Mark Smith Road, turn right (N). Pass some houses. Notice the waterfall to your left just before the "Leaving National Forest" sign.
- This is a steep uphill. Pass the Gorge Trail. The road winds back and forth and continues uphill.
- When the road-dead ends, turn left onto Mathews Road. Pass the Burnt Hill Trail, South Velie Pasture, and a parking area. A communications tower is to your right.
- Head downhill past a sign for Blueberry Patch and Interloken Trail and a parking area.

- At the stop sign, turn right onto Burnt Hill Road. Pass Ravine Trail. The road roller-coasters as it heads north. At the next stop sign, you've come 16.6 miles.
- Turn right onto Picnic Area Road (County Route 2). (To the left is the Red House Country Inn B&B. Straight ahead is Backbone Horse Camp.) Head uphill past Backbone and Interloken Trails.
- At the Blueberry Patch Campground, you may want to take a side trip to pick blueberries if they're in season.
- Pass the Burnt Hill Trail parking area. Pass North Velie Pasture.
- Turn left, and head north on Potomac Road. For 4.0 miles you're retracing a route you took earlier heading south. Pass Chicken Coop Road and County Road 1.
- At the stop sign at Seneca Road, turn right.
- Take the first left onto Case Road/County Road 146.
- In 0.9 mile, turn left onto Townsend Road/County Road 143. Only 2.2 more miles, and you're done.
- Take the first right (N) onto Ames Road, which is a narrow dirt road. Pass Interloken Trail.
- Turn right and head east on Parmenter/Butcher Hill Road. The parking lot is on your right in 0.3 mile.

Date Enjoyed: _____

Notes:

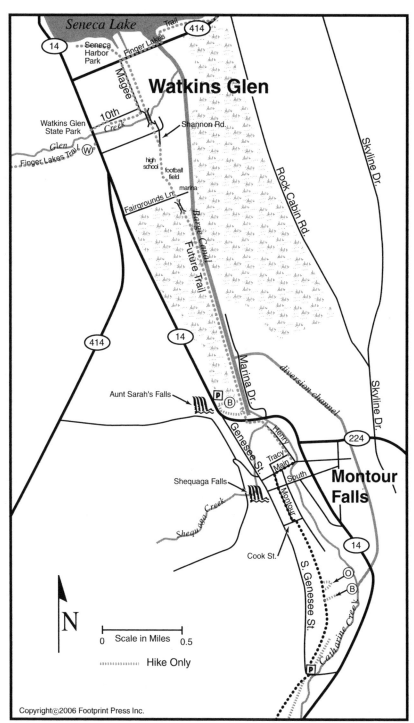

Catharine Valley Trail (North Section)

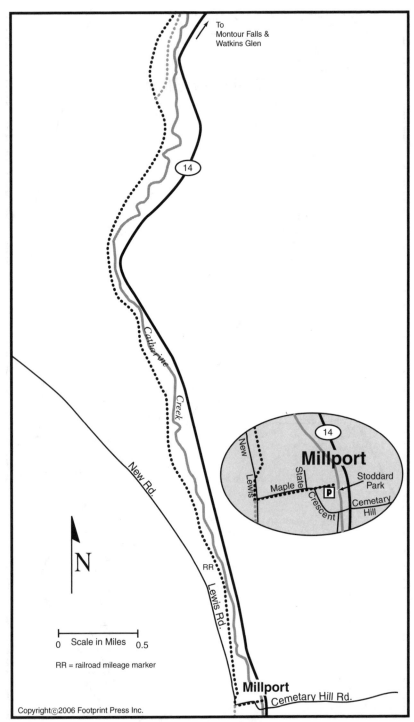

To
Montour Falls &
Watkins Glen

14

Catharine Creek

New Rd.

N

RR

Lewis Rd.

Scale in Miles
0   0.5

RR = railroad mileage marker

Millport

New

Lewis

14

Maple   State

P

Crescent

Stoddard Park

Cemetary Hill

Millport
Cemetary Hill Rd.

Copyright©2006 Footprint Press Inc.

Catharine Valley Trail (Middle Section)

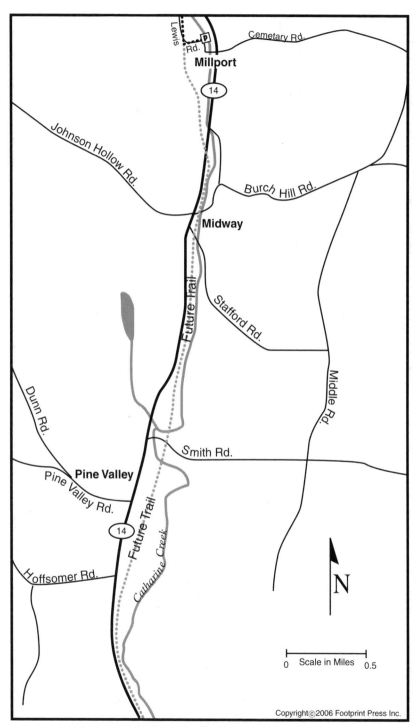

Catharine Valley Trail (Future South Section)

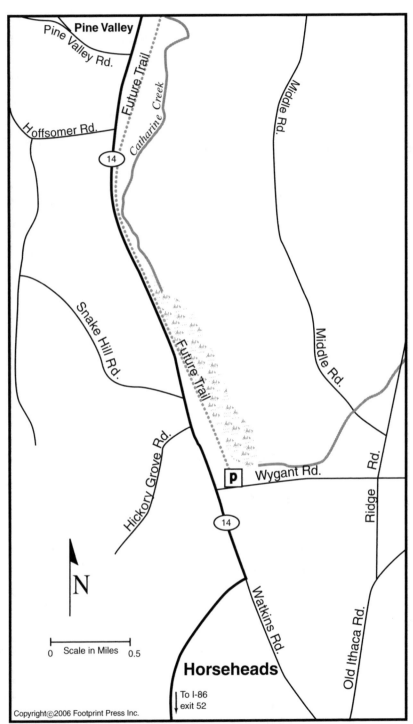

Catharine Valley Trail (Future South End Section)

17.

Catharine Valley Trail

Location: Montour Falls to Millport (eventually Watkins Glen to Horseheads), Schuyler and Chemung Counties. Look for green and white Catharine Valley Trail signs and hiker silhouette signs directing you to parking areas along the trail.

Directions: From Route 14 in Montour Falls, turn west onto Main Street and park along the streets anywhere you find legal parking along Main Street, Montour Street, or Cook Street.

Alternative Parking: South Genesee Street, south of Montour Falls. From the parking lot, the trail is the wide stone dust trail that heads uphill to the north and across South Genesee Street to the south. The dirt path at the back of the lot is a private drive, not part of the trail. N42º 19.720 - W76º 50.657

Alternative Parking: From Route 14 in Millport, turn west onto Crescent Road. At the end, turn right onto Maple Street and park in Stoddard Park at the end of the street. N42º 15.998 - W76º 50.127

Riding Time: 1 hour one way

Length: 6 miles one way

Difficulty: 👣 👣

Surface: Stone dust

Trail Markings: Trailhead signs

Uses:

Dogs: OK on leash no longer than 6 feet

Contact: NYS Office of Parks, Recreation and Historic Preservation
2221 Taughannock Park Road, Trumansburg, NY 14886
(607) 387-7041

Friends of Catharine Valley Trail
www.cvtfriends.elmirampo.org

The Catharine Valley Trail will eventually be a 12-mile-long multi-use trail from Seneca Harbor Park in Watkins Glen to Wygant Road in Hoseheads. As such, it is a work in progress. You may want to call the Finger Lakes State Parks Region office at (607) 387-7041 before heading out to learn about the length of trail currently available. As of 2006, 6 miles of superbly improved trail runs from Montour Falls to Millport. In 2005 a bridge was built over Route 14 south of Millport. 2006 plans include extending the trail south from Millport to the bridge and resurfacing the trail north of Montour Falls. The rest of the trail will come in the

Shequaga Falls in Montour Falls.

future, including connecting it to Seneca Harbor Park in the north and Wygant Road in the south.

New York State Office of Parks, Recreation and Historic Preservation (OPRHP) is responsible for developing the trail. Much of the route follows abandoned Chemung Railroad and Chemung Canal towpath corridors, and those lay largely along old Iroquois trails.

The Chemung Canal, built in 1830, followed the Catharine Creek valley and required 53 locks to lift boats along its 23-mile course from Elmira to Seneca Lake at Watkins Glen. The short canal trip required 2.5 days of travel. To keep the canal afloat in water, a 16-mile-long feeder canal was dug westward to tap the Chemung River at Corning. Built on a shoestring, the canal locks were made of wood rather than stone, and had to be replaced every few years. Floods ripped the canal apart all too frequently and the canal was never enlarged like the Erie Canal was, so it couldn't carry the larger boats. The Chemung Canal was closed in 1878 and emptied south of Montour Falls. During its lifetime, the canal was an important transportation route for lumber, grain, gypsum, whiskey, and pottery.

The Chemung Canal was still in operation when the Chemung Railway was built from Watkins Glen to Elmira, in 1850, on a parallel path. Watch for evidence of both the old railroad and the old canal as you ride the Catharine Valley Trail.

The person responsible for this trail was the late Ed Hoffman, an attorney representing Conrail at the time of the rail line's abandonment. He pitched the notion of converting the land to a trail in the 1970s, long before it was fashionable. He tried again in 1992 when building rail-trails was an active past-time, but no money was available. Ed raised foundation money from several sources, bought the corridor and donated almost 12 miles to OPRHP in 1997. Sadly, Ed died in 1999 just before his 1970s dream became a reality.

The improved trail is covered by a tree canopy in sections and offers quarter mileage markers and benches. From Montour Falls to Millport, there's 5 miles of trail with only one cross street. Ride high above the creek with periodic views through the trees. Watch for the cement marker sporting the number 9 on its south facing side and fifty-some on its north facing side; evidence that this is a former railroad bed. Presumably this denoted 9 miles to Elmira and fifty-some miles to Sodus.

So, just who was Catharine whose valley bears her name? Catharine Montour (est. 1710-1804), part French and part Iroquois, achieved prominence in her matrilineal society due to her ability to translate during

The new Catharine Valley Trail is easy to ride.

negotiations between invading whites and native societies. The "queen" moniker was added by the newcomers. Then, on September 1, 1779, as part of a systematic campaign against the Iroquois, a group of American soldiers, under the direction of Generals Sullivan and Clinton of the Continental Army, attacked a small Iroquoian village in Montour Falls, destroying the Seneca community known as Catharinestown to the whites and She-O-Qua-Gah (land of tumbling waters) to the Indians. Queen Catharine Montour, the clan mother, led her people to safety just hours before the soldiers burned their 30 log homes, adjacent fruit orchards, and winter food stores.

Current trail distance between major roads:

Main Street, Montour Falls to Cook Street	0.3 mile
Cook Street to S. Genesee Street	0.9 mile
Genesee Street to New/Lewis Road, Millport	4.6 miles

Future trail north of Montour Falls:

Seneca Harbor Park, Watkins Glen to Route 414	0.4 mile
Route 414 to Route 14	2.3 miles
Route 14 to Cook Street	0.9 mile

Future trail south of Millport:

New/Lewis Road to Burch Hill Road	1.0 mile
Burch Hill Road to Smith Road	1.4 miles
Smith Road to Wygant Road	3.1 miles

Trail Directions

- From downtown (Main Street) Montour Falls, follow the roads and/or sidewalks south on Montour Street, passing an old railroad station building.
- Turn left onto Cook Street, and watch right for the kiosk marking the start of the improved trail section.
- Turn right onto the wide stone dust trail.
- Pass a hike-only, orange-blazed side loop trail.
- Pass a hike-only, blue-blazed side trail.
- Head downhill to the South Genesee Street parking area. Cross South Genesee Street.
- The trail now splits into an upper and lower route. It doesn't matter which leg you choose, they merge again shortly.
- Continue south on the trail, watch for the railroad milage marker, designated by the RR on the map. N42° 16.531 - W76° 50.390
- Continue south on the trail until it meets New/Lewis Road in Millport.
- Turn left onto New/Lewis Road, then left again onto Maple Street.
- The parking area in Stoddard Park is at the end of Maple Street.

Date Enjoyed: _____

Notes:

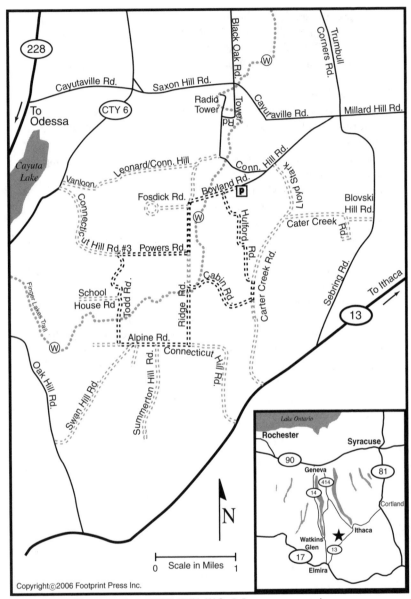

Connecticut Hill Wildlife Management Area

18.

Connecticut Hill Wildlife Management Area

Location: Midway between the south ends of Seneca Lake and Cayuga Lake, 13 miles southwest of Ithaca, Schuyler and Tompkins Counties

Directions: From Ithaca, head south on Route 13. Turn west on Millard Hill Road, 1 mile beyond the junction with Routes 34/96. Pass through Trumbull Corners, then turn left on Connecticut Hill Road. Continue straight onto Boyland Road. Park along the road, near the corner of Boyland Road and Hulford Road. N42° 22.028 - W76° 39.983

Alternative Parking: Anywhere along the roads within the area.

Riding Time: 2 hour loop

Length: 9.1-mile loop

Difficulty:

Surface: Seasonal gravel roads

Trail Markings: None

Uses:

Dogs: OK

Contact: N.Y.S. Department of Environmental Conservation
1285 Fisher Avenue, Cortland, NY 13045
(607) 753-3095   www.dec.state.ny.us

Connecticut Hill is the largest wildlife management area in New York State, covering 11,654 acres. It is part of the Appalachian Highlands, which is distinctive as a belt of high, rough land. Because of this, the area is rugged bicycling. The trail described follows seasonal gravel roads, but the terrain is always hilly, sometimes with steep sections as it winds on and off the plateau. Expect an aerobic workout.

Besides the steep hills, the other challenge of this area is that most roads are not labeled. You need to be able to follow the map and directions to traverse this area successfully. Then too, you'll find that many of the roads are called Connecticut Hill Road, sometimes with a number and sometimes without.

The dirt roads of Connecticut Hill Wildlife Management Area
are hilly but great for biking.

Indians were the first inhabitants to roam this area. They were driven out
by George Washington's troops in the late 1700s. From 1800 until 1850,

the land was owned by the state of Connecticut and then sold to private landowners. However, the name, Connecticut Hill, stuck.

By the mid-19th century, much of the land in this area had been cleared for cultivation and pasture. However, the farms languished due to poor soil conditions, and many farms were abandoned. By 1926, only 20 of the original 109 farms remained in operation. Through the Federal Resettlement Administration, the government began buying farmland and the game refuge came into existence.

Trail Directions
- From the intersection of Boyland Road and Hulford Road, head west on Boyland Road.
- Reach a "T," and turn left (S) onto Ridge Road (also called Connecticut Hill Road).
- Pass Fosdick Road (also called Connecticut Hill Road #2) on the right. At 1.2 miles, turn right (W) onto Connecticut Hill Road #3 (also called Powers Road).
- Take the first left (S) onto Todd Road, and head downhill.
- Turn left to continue south steeply downhill on Todd Road.
- Cross a bridge at 3.1 miles.
- Pass a road on the right, then the crossing of the white-blazed Finger Lakes Trail. Continue gradually downhill.
- Reach a "T," and turn left (E) onto Alpine Road.
- Pass two roads on the right that are close together.
- Pass Summerton Hill Road on the right as you traverse steep hills.
- At 4.9 miles, reach the junction with Ridge Road (Connecticut Hill Road) and turn left (N), heading uphill.
- The white-blazed Finger Lakes Trail will cross the road.
- At Cabin Road, turn right (E). Ride a steep downhill, then emerge to open fields.
- At 7.2 miles, turn left (N) on Carter Creek Road.
- Cross Carter Creek.
- 0.2 mile after crossing Carter Creek, turn left (W) onto Hulford Road. Head uphill for a while and then the road will level out.
- Reach Boyland Road and turn right to find your car.

    Date Enjoyed: _____

    Notes:

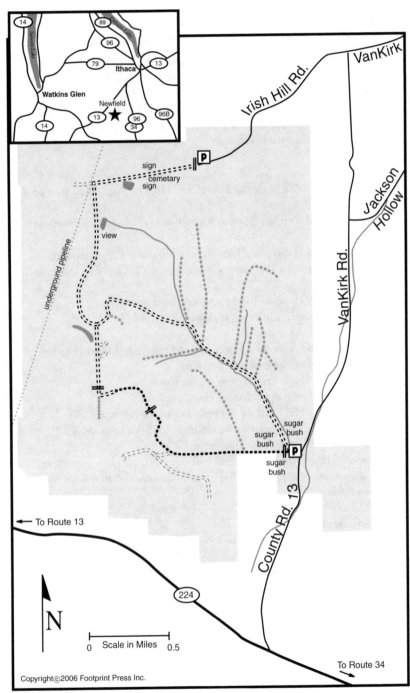

14

89 *Cayuga Lake*

96

79 **Ithaca** 13

Seneca Lake

Watkins Glen

Newfield ★

14 13 96 96B

34

Irish Hill Rd. VanKirk

P

sign

cemetary
sign

view

underground pipeline

VanKirk Rd.

Jackson Hollow

sugar
bush

sugar
bush

sugar
bush

P

← To Route 13

County Rd. 13

224

N

Scale in Miles
0   0.5

To Route 34

Arnot Forest

19.

Arnot Forest

Location:	Newfield, Tompkins County
Directions:	From Ithaca, take Route 13 west and exit at Newfield. Turn right on Main Street, then south on VanKirk Road at the sign for "Arnot Forest." Continue south on VanKirk Road at a left turn, to the brown, wooden sign "Cornell University — Arnot Teaching & Research Forest" on the right.

Alternative parking: Before the gate at the end of Irish Hill Road.
N42° 17.632 - W76° 38.535

Surface:	Dirt roads and grassy trails
Trail Markings:	None
Uses:	
Dogs:	OK on leash
Contact:	Forest Manager, Department of Natural Resources
	Cornell University
	611 County Route 13, VanEtten, NY 14889
	(607) 589-6095 www.dnr.cornell.edu/arnot/

The adventure begins in the village of Newfield where you'll pass the only remaining covered bridge still in daily use in New York State. The Newfield Bridge was built in 1853 over Cayuga Inlet Creek.

Then on to the 4,000-acre Arnot Teaching and Research Forest. It is owned by Cornell University and is used for student fieldwork, research, and extension activities. The forest is home to many ongoing demonstration projects and an active springtime maple sugaring operation. Once abandoned farmland and wood lots, Cornell University has owned this land since the 1920s. The public is welcome to explore the dirt roads and trails, but please stay out of posted or restricted areas.

The trails are mostly dead-ends, little used and little maintained. For biking, its best to stay on the tree-shaded dirt roads that wind through the property. The high elevation point of this land is Irish Hill Road. You can either park before the barrier along Irish Hill Road and ride downhill to the parking area off VanKirk Road, or do a round trip, riding uphill from VanKirk Road to Irish Hill and back down again.

This land is an active hunting forest so please avoid biking during hunting season. The cemetery along Irish Hill Roads dates to the early 1800s.

Blue tubes wind through the forest, connecting sugar maple trees for gathering sap to make maple syrup.

Downhill from Irish Hill Road

Riding Time: 35 minutes one way
Length: 4.3 miles one way
Difficulty: 👣 👣

Trail Directions:
- From the gate at the end of Irish Hill Road head west on the dirt road.
- Pass the 1800s cemetery on the left.
- Pass large brown signs on each side of the road for "Woodland Wildlife Demonstration Project."
- Turn left onto a dirt road.
- Pass a pond and panoramic view to your left.
- Continue downhill.
- Stay on the main road, passing a road to the right and many side trails.

•As the road winds downhill through the valley, it will cross the creek several times.
•Notice the blue tubes connecting the sugar maple trees and a sugar house shortly before reaching the parking area at VanKirk Road.

Date Enjoyed: _____

Notes:

The dirt roads in Arnot Forest offer solitude.

Loop from VanKirk Road

Riding Time: 50 minute loop
Length: 4.8-mile loop
Difficulty: 👣 👣 👣 👣

Trail Directions

•From the parking area off VanKirk Road, head uphill on the wide dirt road.
•Notice the blue tubes connecting the sugar maple trees and a sugar house.
•Stay on the main road, heading uphill, passing many side trails.
•Turn left onto a side road
•Begin downhill.
•Pass two gates. The road will turn to trail.
•Follow it downhill, passing another gate just before meeting the main road.
•Turn left onto the main road to return to the parking area.

Date Enjoyed: _____

Notes:

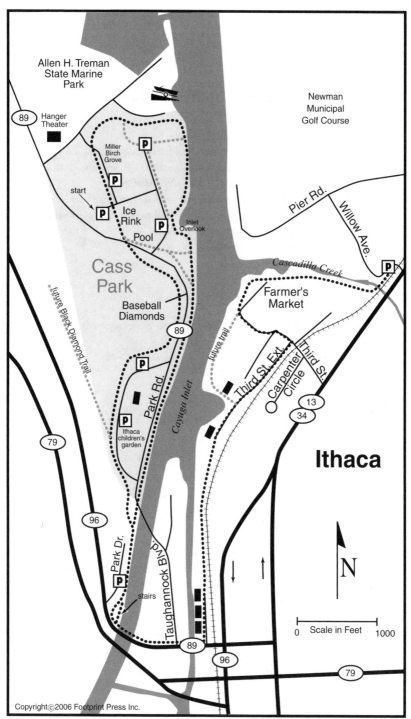

Cayuga Waterfront Trail

20.

Cayuga Waterfront Trail

Location:	Ithaca, Tompkins County
Directions:	From Route 89, north of Ithaca, turn into Cass Park at the pool. Turn left to pass the ice rink and park at the end. N42º 27.197 - W76º 30.916

Alternative Parking: Lots of other parking areas within Cass Park.

Alternative Parking: A small pull-off along Willow Avenue (off Route 13/34) and the railroad tracks, at the end of the trail. N42º 27.080 - W76º 30.245

Riding Time:	50 minute loop
Length:	5.5-mile loop
Difficulty:	
Surface:	Paved trails in Cass Park and gravel segments east of Cayuga Inlet.
Trail Markings:	None
Uses:	
Dogs:	OK on leash
Contact:	The Cayuga Waterfront Trail Initiative
	(60) 592-4647
	www.cayugawaterfronttrail.com
	The City of Ithaca
	Tompkins County Chamber of Commerce Foundation 904 East Shore Drive, Ithaca, NY 14850 (607) 273-7080

The Cayuga Waterfront Trail is a work in progress. It will eventually run for 6 miles along the Cayuga Lake Shore and connect to the future 15-mile-long Black Diamond Trail. The section east of Cayuga Inlet is slated for improvement in 2007. Pick up a copy of the brochure "The Cayuga Waterfront Trail Walk Through History" from boxes along the trail, for a more detailed description of the history of the Cass Park area.

Today you can ride a 2-mile loop on paved trails through Cass Park or ride an 5.5-mile loop trip by heading out from Cass Park and continuing on the gravel trail on the east side of Cayuga Inlet to Willow Avenue and back. It's an easy ride with waterfront scenery.

Trail Directions
- From Cass Park, near the ice rink, head south on the paved trail.
- Pass a connector trail to the left.
- Carefully cross Route 89.
- As the trail bends around the baseball diamonds (Union Fields) you're riding on the northernmost curve of the Lehigh Valley Railroad turnaround which circled the freight yards.
- At mileage marker 0.5 look north along the power lines . This will be the site of the Black Diamond Trail.
- At the trail junction, turn right to continue south.
- Bear right to go up a ramp to the Route 96 sidewalk. (If you continue straight, you'll encounter stairs.)
- Continue to the left, crossing the Route 96 bridge on the sidewalk.
- Continue straight over a second bridge.
- At the first road turn left and ride through a business district.
- Continue straight on the gravel path, with railroad tracks to your right.
- Continue straight when the road (Third Street Extension) turns to pavement.
- At the end, turn left onto Third Street.
- At the Farmer's Market, bear left on the dirt path, close to the Inlet.
- The path will curve around, following Cascadilla Creek and will end at the parking pull-off on Willow Avenue.
- Turn around and retrace your path back through the Farmer's Market, out to Route 89 and over two bridges.
- Head right down the ramp on the west side of Cayuga Inlet.
- This time bear right at the next trail junction to ride along Cayuga Inlet.
- Cross Route 89 through an underpass. Watch right for rowers in Cayuga Inlet. It's a sport that has flourished here since the early 1870s.
- Continue north past an overlook, several benches, and paths to the left.
- The path will bend left and cross a park road.
- When you ride through the young birch trees in Miller Grove, you're on the site of Ithaca's first airport, built in 1914 by the Thomas Brothers. The Hangar Theater in Cass Park was a concrete hangar built in 1932.
- Cross another park road to return to the starting parking lot.

Date Enjoyed: _____

Notes:

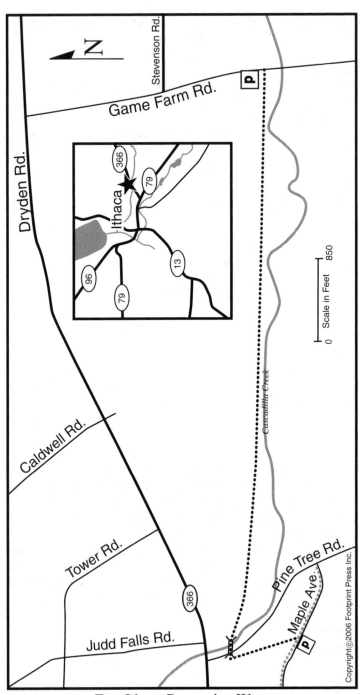

East Ithaca Recreation Way

21.

East Ithaca Recreation Way

Location:	Ithaca, Tompkins County
Directions:	From Ithaca follow Route 366 east. Turn south on Game Farm Road. The parking area is on the west side of Game Farm Road, 0.6 mile from Route 366. Watch for the green-and-white, square bicycle signs. N42o 26.481 - W76o 26.922
Alternative Parking:	On the south side of Maple Avenue. N42o 26.456 - W76o 28.203
Riding Time:	20 minutes round trip
Length:	2.2 miles round trip
Difficulty:	
Surface:	Paved trail
Trail Markings:	Wooden mile marker signs every quarter mile
Uses:	
Dogs:	OK on leash
Contact:	Cornell Plantations One Plantation Road, Ithaca, NY 14850-2799 (607) 255-3020

Here's an easy trail for beginners or families with young children. It's a short trail with scenic views of a creek along the way. To avoid the short steep section, turn around at the Cascadilla Creek bridge. Alternatively, to lengthen the ride, continue on the paved trail parallel to Maple Avenue.

Trail Directions
- From the parking area on Game Farm Road, head west on the paved trail.
- Cascadilla Creek will be to your left.
- At 1.0 mile, cross Cascadilla Creek and Pine Tree Road on bridges.
- The paved trail bends sharply left and heads uphill.
- At 1.1 miles, reach Maple Avenue.
- Turn around and retrace your path back to Game Farm Road.

    Date Enjoyed: _____

    Notes:

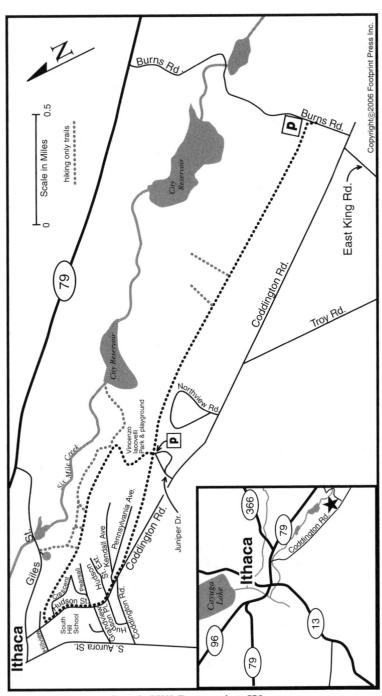

South Hill Recreation Way

22.

South Hill Recreation Way

Location:	Ithaca, Tompkins County
Directions:	From Ithaca follow Route 79 east. Turn right (S) on Burns Road. Parking is on the west side of Burns Road at a sign for "South Hill Recreation Way Parking." Watch for the green-and-white, square bicycle signs. N42º 24.298 - W76º 27.688
Alternative Parking:	At the end of Juniper Drive. N42º 25.417 - W76º 28.917
Riding Time:	1 hour loop
Length:	6-mile loop
Difficulty:	
Surface:	Packed gravel trail and a short paved section, sidewalk along Hudson Street.
Trail Markings:	Yellow-and-brown wooden signs "South Hill Recreation Way" and mile marker signs every half mile
Uses:	
Dogs:	OK on leash
Contact:	Town of Ithaca Highway/Parks Department 106 Seven Mile Drive, Ithaca, NY 14850 (607) 273-8035

This trail was developed in 1986 as a N.Y.S. Environmental Quality Bond Act Project. It follows the abandoned rail bed of the Cayuga and Susquehanna, which was built in 1849 to haul anthracite coal from the Pennsylvania mines to a canal in Ithaca. Eventually it merged with the Delaware, Lackawanna, and Western Railroad and was abandoned in 1957.

The terrain is gradual hills, mostly downhill on the outbound leg and uphill for the return. You're riding in the Six Mile Creek Gorge. This creek is currently dammed for use as a water supply for Ithaca. Hiking paths lead off the biking trail into the gorge. Numbered posts are positioned along part of the route at the western end. Brochures that explain the plant communities you'll pass are available along the trail. Here's a synopsis:

1. Weedy Invasives – European honeysuckle in bush form grows here.
2. Tree of Heaven – This tree was imported from China as a hardy tree that can withstand harsh urban conditions.
3. Shagbark Hickory – A native tree with shaggy, pealing gray bark.
4. Goldenrod – Its bright yellow flowers are a sign of fall.
5. Black Locust – A tree with sweet-smelling flowers in spring and compound elliptical leaflets.
6. Cottonwood – Also known as poplar or quaking aspen, this is a fast growing tree.
7. Black Walnut – A tree prized for its wood.
8. Fossils – Look for the marine animals that once inhabited the shallow sea that covered this area.
9. Simple and Vascular Plants – Moss and wild geraniums grow on the rocks behind you.
10. Old Growth Forest – These trees are 75 to 100 years old or older.
11. Non-Native Species of a Different Sort – The unusual stones here are glacial erratics that were brought south by the glaciers.
12. Old Farm Fields – 50 years ago, this area of small trees was a farm field.

The side trails you'll pass are for pedestrians only.

Trail Directions
- From the Burns Road trail entrance, head downhill.
- At 1.7 miles, pass Juniper Drive. Parking is available here.
- Pass a trail to the right, to Vincenzo Iacovelli Park.
- Reach Coddinton Road at 2.3 miles.
- Turn right and follow the sidewalk downhill.
- After passing Crescent Street, turn right onto trail again. (N42º 26.090 - W76º 29.516)
- Watch for the numbered posts that describe the plant communities in the Six Mile Creek Gorge.
- Head uphill on the paved part of the trail into Vincenzo Iacovelli Park.
- Turn left at the "T."
- Pass Juniper Drive.
- Reach Burns Road.

A sign marks the end of South Hill Recreation Way.

Date Enjoyed: _____

Notes:

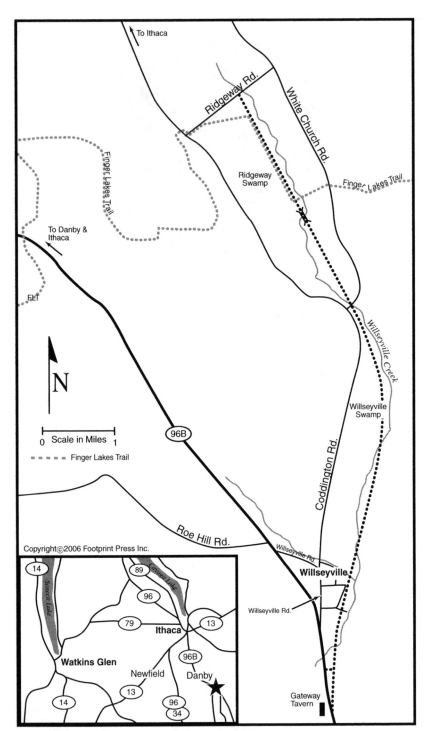

Ridgeway Trail

23.

Ridgeway Trail

Location:	Willseyville, Tompkins County
Directions:	From Ithaca, head south on Route 96B to Willseyville. Turn left onto Willseyville Road, then left (N) again onto Coddington Road. Turn right (E) onto Ridgeway Road. Park along the road, near the trailhead. N42° 20.476 - W76° 23.434
Alternative Parking:	The Gateway Tavern parking lot on Route 96B in Willseyville. N42° 16.893 - W76° 22.697 The trail is a farm lane at this end, between houses #907 and 895.
Riding Time:	45 minutes one way
Length:	4.7 miles one way
Difficulty:	
Surface:	Cinder double-track
Trail Markings:	None
Uses:	
Dogs:	OK on leash
Contact:	Tompkins County Greenway Coalition 1456 Hanshaw Road, Ithaca, NY 14850-2754 (607) 257-6220

Ride this rail-trail through Ridgeway Swamp and Willseyville Swamp, through the valley of Willseyville Creek. The railbed is the old Delaware and Lackawanna Railroad, Ithaca's earliest railroad, built in 1937. It featured an inclined rail lift up South Hill. The last train rumbled through here in 1956. Now the crushed cinder base makes a nice biking surface.

The Finger Lakes Trail uses the northern section of the Ridgeway Trail then veers off to the east. Other than the small segment where the two trails co-exist, the Finger Lakes Trail is for hiking only.

Trail Directions
•From Ridgeway Road, head south on the cinder trail. White blazes will show that this segment is also the Finger Lakes Trail.

- Continue straight as the Finger Lakes Trail heads east. (N42º 19.734 - W76º 22.614)
- Cross Willseyville Creek on a bridge.
- Cross White Church Road.
- Pass behind the village of Willseyville.
- The trail ends at Route 96B across from the Gateway Tavern.

Date Enjoyed: _____

Notes:

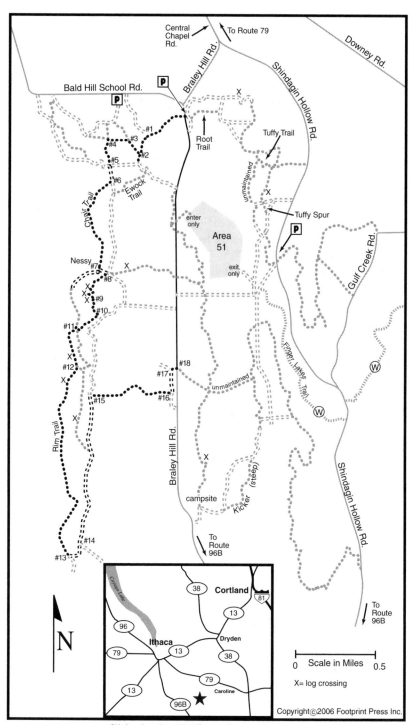

Central Chapel Rd.

To Route 79

Downey Rd.

Bald Hill School Rd.

P

P

Braley Hill Rd.

Shindagin Hollow Rd.

X

#1
#3
#4
#2
#5
#6

Root Trail

Tuffy Trail

Ewock Trail

Chair Trail

unmaintained

enter only

Area 51

exit only

Tuffy Spur

P

Gulf Creek Rd.

Nessy
#7
#8
X
X
X
X
#9
#10

#11

W

Finger Lakes Trail

W

X
#12
X

#18
#17
#16
#15

unmaintained

Braley Hill Rd.

Rim Trail

X

Shindagin Hollow Rd.

X

campsite

Kicker (steep)

To Route 96B

#14
#13

To Route 96B

Cayuga Lake

38

Cortland

81

13

96

Ithaca

13

Dryden

79

38

79

13

Caroline

96B

★

N

Scale in Miles

0   0.5

X= log crossing

Copyright©2006 Footprint Press Inc.

Shindagin Hollow State Forest

24.

Shindagin Hollow State Forest

Location: Caroline, Tompkins County

Directions: Take Route 79 east from Ithaca to Slaterville Springs. Just after Caroline Elementary School, turn right onto Boiceville Road. At the "T," turn left onto Valley Road /Central Chapel Road. At the "Y," bear right on Braley Hill Road. Watch for the parking area, 0.5 mile south of the "Y," on the left.   N42° 20.796 - W76° 20.975

Alternative Parking: Bald Hill School Road.   N42° 20.825 - W76° 21.419

Alternative Parking: Shindagin Hollow Road, 1.5 mile south of the "Y," on the left.   N42° 19.935 - W76° 20.393

Riding Time: 30 minute loop

Length: 2.9-mile loop

Difficulty: 👣 👣 👣 👣 (mountain biking)

Surface: Dirt single-track and double-track trails, plus logging and fire roads.

Trail Markings: None

Uses: 🚶 🚴 ⛷ 🏃

Dogs: OK on leash

Contact: NYS Department of Environmental Conservation
Caroline, NY
(607) 753-3095   www.dec.state.ny.us

Shindagin Hollow is the domain of rugged mountain bikers. The miles of challenging single-track are not for the faint of heart — or faint of suspension. You'll find roots and rocks galore, steep climbs, and unforgiving descents. It's easy to get lost here, and a wrong turn can mean a long ride back to your car. The white-blazed Finger Lakes Trail winds through this forest and is for hiking only.

Area 51 is a zone for technical riding by experienced mountain bikers only. It was built as a one-way trail,-+ so please use the north entrance. Inside you'll find elevated obstacles, teeter-totters, log bridges, log rides and ride-off jumps.

The ride described is an intermediate level mountain biking loop that offers a mixture of single-track, double-track, logging roads, fire roads, and a cool down return on Braley Hill Road. Intersections are numbered on the map and in the directions to facilitate route finding. For some more extensive (and even more challenging) mountain biking rides in Shindagin Hollow State Forest, pick up a copy of the *Shindagin Hollow Braley Hill Trail Guide* ($7) at any area bike shop.

Trail Directions

- From the Braley Road parking area, head west on the double-track trail.
- At the first junction (1) turn left onto single-track trail.
- At the next intersection (2) turn right, uphill.
- Bear left at the "Y" (3).
- Turn left, heading downhill (4).
- At the bottom, turn left onto a fire road, then take a quick right onto another fire road (5).
- Take the second right onto a single-track called Chair Trail (6).
- Turn left onto double-track (7) at a log ride called Nessy.
- Turn right onto a single-track trail (8) and cross 3 log crossings.
- Turn left onto double-track trail (9).
- Turn right onto double-track trail (10). Then, turn right onto double-track, which will narrow to single-track.
- Go straight through intersection 11.
- Stay right to follow the Rim Trail (12).
- Stay left past intersections 13 and 14, onto a fire road.
- Turn right onto double-track trail (15). Pass through a pine forest then a steep downhill with a tight left turn at the bottom.
- Turn left onto double-track (16).
- Turn right onto a narrow double-track trail (17).
- At Braley Hill Road (18) turn left, and follow the road 1.5 miles back to the parking area.

Date Enjoyed: _____

Notes:

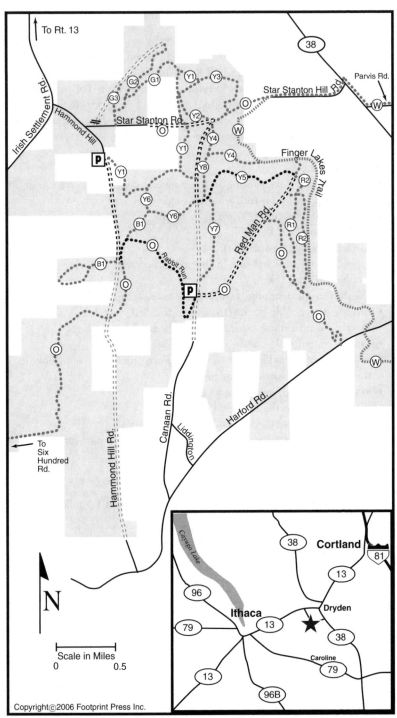

Hammond Hill State Forest

25.

Hammond Hill State Forest

Location:	Dryden and Caroline, Tompkins County
Directions:	From Ithaca, head east on Route 13. Pass Yellow Barn Hill Road, and turn south on Irish Settlement Road. Turn left (E) on Hammond Hill Road. Follow it to the end. N42° 26.211 - W76° 18.322
Riding Time:	1 hour loop
Length:	6.1-mile loop (darkened trail)
	10.4 miles of total trails for biking
Difficulty:	👣 👣 👣 👣 (mountain biking)
Surface	Woods trails, dirt double-track roads
Trail Markings:	Numbered trail junctions, round plastic markers (colored and numbered)
Uses:	🚶 🚴 🎿 🏃 🐎 🛷
Dogs:	OK
Contact:	NYS Department of Environmental Conservation
	1285 Fisher Avenue, Cortland, NY 13045
	(607) 753-3095 ext. 215 www.dec.state.ny.us

Hammond Hill was established as a state forest between 1935 and 1950 in an effort to reduce soil erosion, produce forest products, and provide recreational opportunities. Once depleted farmland, it was planted with thousands of pine, spruce, larch, maple, ash, cherry, and oak seedlings. Today the 3,618 acres are forested to support management activities.

Sitting above 1,800 feet in elevation, the network of trails are an active place for fun in winter as well as the other seasons. The 10.4 miles of yellow, blue, red, and green trails are for hiking, cross-country skiing, snowshoeing, mountain biking, and horseback riding. 5.6 miles of orange trails are designated for snowmobiling in winter, but allow hiking and biking the rest of the year. The white-blazed Finger Lakes Trail crosses through Hammond Hill State Forest. It is designated for hiking and snowshoeing only.

The route described below mainly uses dirt roads through this hilly terrain. It's a challenging ride, but it's less so than a route on the woods trails.

If you want a rugged mountain biking experience, use the map to pick a trail ride — just please stay off the white-blazed Finger Lakes Trail.

Yellow Trails - 5.6 miles on old logging roads and fire lanes

Trail	Level of Difficulty	Distance
Y1	Moderate	1.9 miles
Y2	Easy	0.6 mile
Y3	Moderate (scenic view of Dryden Lake)	0.6 mile
Y4	Moderate	1.0 mile

Trail	Level of Difficulty	Distance
Y4B	Moderate	0.1 mile
Y5	Difficult	1.3 miles
Y6	Easy	0.2 mile
Y7	Difficult	1.0 mile

Blue Trail - 1.4 miles

Trail	Level of Difficulty	Distance
B1	Moderate	1.4 miles

Red Trails - 1.7 miles

Trail	Level of Difficulty	Distance
R1	Difficult	0.6 mile
R2	Difficult	1.1 miles

Green Snowmobile Trails - 5.6 miles

Trail	Level of Difficulty	Distance
G1	Difficult	0.8 mile
G2	Moderate	0.7 mile
G3	Difficult	0.2 mile

Finger Lakes Trail (white blazes)   3.2 miles (Hiking Only)

Orange Snowmobile Trail (Forest Access and Seasonal Use Roads), 5.6 miles

Trail Directions

- From the parking area at the northern end of Hammond Hill Road, head south on dirt Hammond Hill Road.
- At the junction turn left onto Blue 1 (B1). (It will co-exist with the orange snowmobile trail for a short distance.
- When the two diverge, bear right on the orange trail (Rabbit Run).
- When you reach dirt Canaan Road, turn left then a quick right onto dirt Red Man Road, still following orange blazes.
- When the orange trail leaves Red Man Road, continue straight on the dirt road.
- At the end, turn left onto Yellow 5 (Y5) trail.
- Pass yellow 7 & 8 trails, and turn right onto Canaan Road.
- At the end, turn left onto dirt Star Stanton Road.

•Star Stanton Road becomes paved. At the end, turn left onto Hammond Hill Road, and follow it back to the parking area.

Date Enjoyed: _____

Notes:

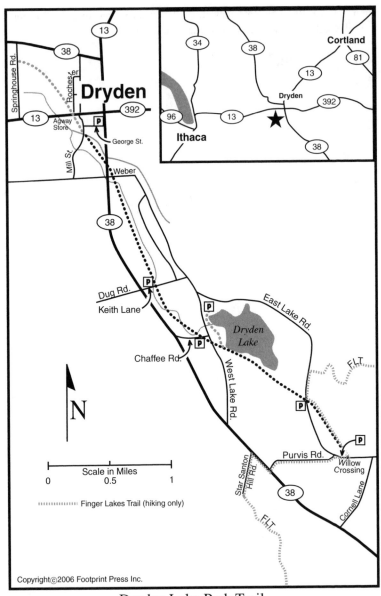

Dryden Lake Park Trail

26.

Dryden Lake Park Trail

Location:	Dryden, east of Ithaca, Tompkins and Cortland Counties
Directions:	From Ithaca follow Route 13 east to Dryden. Turn right (S) on Route 38 and right (W) again onto George Street. Look for the parking lot on the right. N42° 29.391 - W76° 17.894

Alternative Parking: Keith Lane. N42° 28.158 - W76° 17.364
Alternative Parking: Chaffee Road. N42° 27.763 - W76° 16.865
Alternative Parking: Dryden Lake Park on West Lake Road.
   N42° 27.880 - W76° 16.772
Alternative Parking: East Lake Road. N42° 27.258 - W76° 15.731
Alternative Parking: Willow Crossing. N42° 26.827 - W76° 15.276

Riding Time:	1.2 hours round trip
Length:	7.7 miles round trip
Difficulty:	🥾
Surface:	Mowed grass and packed gravel trail
Trail Markings:	Square blue-and-white metal signs "Dryden Lake Park Trail," and mile markers every half mile along the trail
Uses:	
Dogs:	OK on leash
Contact:	Town of Dryden
	65 East Main Street, Dryden, NY 13053
	(607) 844-8619 www.dryden.ny.us

The Southern Central Railroad was built in 1865 to connect Sayre, Pennsylvania to Auburn. It became part of the Lehigh Valley System and was abandoned in 1976. The tracks were taken up and sold for scrap in 1979.

The Agway, along the trail in Dryden, was once the location of a private feed mill. Later, local farmers established a cooperative called the "Farmers Feed and Milling Corporation." GLF (which became Agway) modernized the grain mill in the 1930s.

Dryden Lake Park is 0.1 mile north of the West Lake Road crossing. This park offers fishing access, picnic tables and a pavilion, rest rooms, a

Dryden Lake Park Trail.

playground, and an observation deck over the lake. The area was once an Indian campground and home of an early sawmill (washed away in the flood of 1902) and railroad ice station.

Interpretive signs along this easy-riding trail offer information on the animals and plants that inhabit the area. Birds are abundant, and beaver activity is evident if you watch carefully.

Trail Directions
•From the George Street parking lot, head right (W) on George Street.
•Turn left (S) onto Mill Street.
•Cross the creek bridge and the trail will be to your left. Turn left onto the trail. (To the north the trail ends in 0.8 mile at Springhouse Road.)

- Cross busy Route 38, then quickly cross Weber Street.
- Pass a 1-mile marker and bench. A swamp is on the right.
- Cross Keith Lane. (Parking is available here.)
- Pass a 2-mile marker and bench.
- Cross Chaffee Road. (Parking is available here.)
- Cross West Lake Road. Dryden Lake Park (with parking) is a short distance to the left.
- Pass a deck overlooking Dryden Lake.
- Pass a 3-mile marker and bench.
- Cross East Lake Road. (Parking is available here.)
- Pass a 4-mile marker and bench.
- The trail ends at a parking area on Willow Crossing. Turn around and retrace your path.

Date Enjoyed: _____

Notes:

The authors, Rich & Sue Freeman, have written 14 guidebooks
covering all aspects of outdoor recreation
in central and western New York State.
Peruse their full offerings at www.footprintpress.com.

Rides in Cayuga, Onondaga, Cortland and Wayne Counties

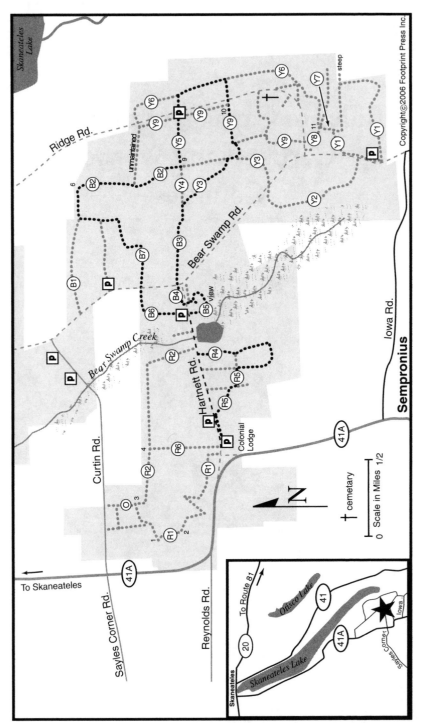

Bear Swamp State Forest

27.

Bear Swamp State Forest

Location: At the southwest end of Skaneateles Lake, Cayuga County

Directions: From Skaneateles, head south on Route 41A. Pass Curtin Road and Reynolds Road. Turn left on the next unmarked dirt road. A brown and yellow D.E.C. sign is on the right side of Route 41A, "Bear Swamp State Forest." Park along the dirt road where you see a wooden kiosk at the trailhead on the left side of the road. N42º 44.933 - W76º 2030

Alternative Parking: Hartnett Road, across from Trail R5.
N42º 45.278 - W76º 19.034

Alternative Parking: Hartnett Road, across from Trail B6.
N42º 45.101 - W76º 18.130

Alternative Parking: Curtin Road, no trails nearby.
N42º 45.601 - W76º 18.624

Alternative Parking: Curtin Road, across from Trail B1.
N42º 45.773 - W76º 18.361

Alternative Parking: Bear Swamp Road, between Trails B1 & B7.
N42º 45.508 - W76º 17.974

Alternative Parking: Bear Swamp Road, near Trail Y1.
N42º 44.180 - W76º 17.106

Alternative Parking: Ridge Road, near Trail Y5.
N42º 44.881 - W76º 16.713

Riding Time: 2 hour loop

Length: 7.2-mile loop

Difficulty: 👣 👣 👣 (mountain biking)

Surface: Single-track and double-track dirt trails and fire roads.

Trail Markings: Two-inch round yellow disks with black lettering, "NYS Environmental Conservation Ski Trail." Also, many intersections have six-inch brown signs with yellow numbers posted on trees above head level.

Uses:

Dogs: OK

Contact: N.Y.S. Department of Environmental Conservation
P.O. Box 5170, Fisher Road, Cortland, NY 13045-5170
(607) 753-3095   www.dec.state.ny.us

This 3,316-acre state forest is traversed with 13 miles of trails through shady forest — enough to keep an avid mountain biker busy all day without backtracking. Over 10,000 years ago, the glaciers sculpted the Finger Lakes, leaving steep valley walls and flat-topped ridges. Native Americans used this area as hunting grounds. After the Revolutionary War, veterans and their families cleared the forests and settled the area. Farming continued through the Civil War and slowly declined as the soil was depleted, until the Great Depression of 1929 hastened farm abandonment. As with the other State Forest land, this land was purchased in the 1930s and was replanted by the Civilian Conservation Corps with red pine, Norway spruce, and larch. You'll be passing through these replanted forests, now a mix of conifers and hardwoods.

Bear Swamp State Forest is managed using the multiple-use concept. This includes maintaining wildlife habitat, harvesting wood products, and encouraging recreational uses. The roads in Bear Swamp State Forest are rough but navigable by a vehicle. They are seasonal use roads that are not plowed in the winter.

The trails are well marked with round, yellow ski trail markers. When in doubt, follow the marked trail. The trails are muddy in spring and after a rain, but summer and fall offer great biking. Some trails are narrow and have roots to traverse, but others are wide, with hard packed dirt providing easy riding. Hills tend to be long, but not particularly steep (with a few exceptions).

Trail Directions
•From Hartnett Road parking (near Route 41A), head east on Hartnett Road.
•Turn right onto Trail R5 and head uphill.
•Pass an intersection and continue east of R5.
•At the next intersection turn right.
•The trail will round a bend than meet Trail R4. Follow Trail R4 downhill.
•Turn right onto Hartnett Road. Head downhill, cross Bear Swamp Creek, then head uphill.
•At a parking area, turn left onto Trail B6, and continue uphill.
•Cross Bear Swamp Road, and continue heading east on Trail B7.
•Pass a trail to the left, then turn left onto Trail B2.
•Pass Trail Y6 (unmaintained), then turn left onto Trail Y5.

- Cross Ridge Road.
- When Trail Y5 ends, turn right onto Trail Y6.
- At the next intersection, turn right onto Trail Y9.
- Cross Ridge Road, then pass intersection 10.
- Turn right at the next intersection.
- Continue straight at the next intersection onto Trail Y3.
- Turn left onto Trail B3.
- Cross Bear Swamp Road.
- Follow Trail B4 down to Hartnett Road.
- Cross Hartnett Road, and take Trail B5 for a short, easy loop to see a pretty view overlooking the Bear Swamp Creek swamp.
- Back at Hartnett Road, turn left, and follow the road to your car.

Date Enjoyed: _____

Notes:

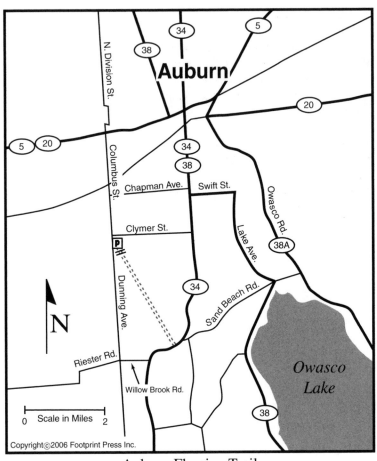

Auburn-Fleming Trail

28.

Auburn – Fleming Trail

Location:	South of Auburn, Cayuga County
Directions:	From Route 5 & 20, turn south on Columbus Street. Parking is on the east side of Dunning Avenue, south of Clymer Street. It is marked by a brown sign with yellow lettering "Cayuga County Trail, Auburn – Fleming" N42° 54.824 - W76° 35.024
Riding Time:	30 minutes round trip
Length:	3.2 miles round trip
Difficulty:	
Surface:	Dirt and cinder trail
Trail Markings:	None
Uses:	
Dogs:	OK
Contact:	County Planner
	Cayuga County Planning Board
	160 Genesee Street, Auburn, NY 13021-1276
	(315) 253-1276
	Cayuga County Parks and Trails Commission
	East Lake Road, Auburn, N.Y. 13021
	(315) 253-5611
	www.co.cayuga.ny.us/parks/trails/aub-fleming.html

The Auburn – Fleming Trail uses an abandoned railroad bed. There's not much elevation change, but the terrain roller coasters and is populated with enough deteriorating railroad ties to make the ride interesting. It's a pleasant walk or ride in a four-foot-wide tunnel of trees.

Trail Directions
- The trail begins behind (W) the sign, with a rough ride over old wooden ties buried in the ground.
- After 0.25 mile, cross a stream on a metal grate bridge.
- A marsh will be on the left. Cross its outlet over a wooden railroad tie bridge.
- The ride now gets smoother.

- Cross a second railroad tie bridge.
- Unmarked trails lead off to the left. (Please stay on the Auburn – Fleming Trail. The trails to the left are on private property.) Continue straight.
- There's a dip in the trail and then a farm lane crossing.
- Cross another railroad tie bridge over a creek. The trail begins to undulate up and down like a roller coaster.
- A trail to the right heads to a farm.
- Pass some small side loops carved by mountain bikers.
- The trail ends at Route 34. Turn around and retrace your path.

Date Enjoyed: _____

Notes:

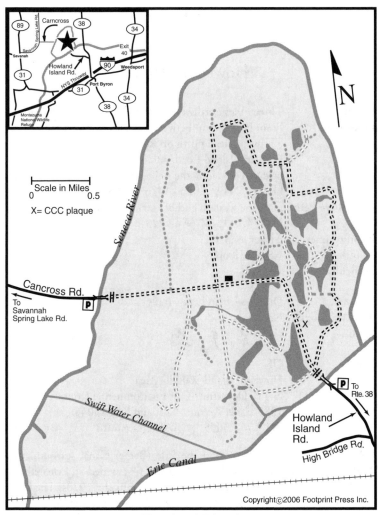

Howland Island

29.

Howland Island

Location:	Three miles northwest of Port Byron, Cayuga County
Directions:	From Port Byron (between exits 40 & 41 on the N.Y.S. Thruway) head north on Route 38. Turn west on Howland Island Road, and follow it to the closed bridge. Park along the right side of the road, before the bridge. N42° 4.020 - W76° 40.033

Alternative Parking: At the western end of Cancross Road.
N43° 4.700 - W76° 42.223

Riding Time:	2 hour loop
Length:	7.8-mile loop
Difficulty:	🥾 🥾 🥾
Surface:	Dirt, gravel, and grass trails
Trail Markings:	None
Uses:	🚶 🚴 🎿 🏃
Dogs:	OK
Contact:	Howland Island Wildlife Area
	N.Y.S. Department Of Environmental Conservation
	1285 Fisher Avenue, Cortland, NY 13045
	(607) 753-3095 www.dec.state.ny.us

Waters of the Seneca River and the Erie (Barge) Canal surround the 3,100 acres of Howland Island. The land was first settled and cleared for farming in the 1800s, and farming continued until the 1920s. The land was purchased as a game refuge in 1932, and became a Civilian Conservation Corps (C.C.C.) camp between 1933 and 1941. The C.C.C. built 18 earthen dikes to create about 300 acres of water impoundments.

The rolling hills and steep drumlins above these impoundments are now home to a second growth mixture of hardwoods, such as maple, ash, willow, basswood, black locust, oak, and hickory. The trails are abandoned gravel roads and old service vehicle tracks, now sufficiently packed to make pleasant biking trails. The route described here uses gravel roads for the predominately uphill section and packed grass trails for the predominately downhill section.

A family enjoys biking on the old roads on Howland Island.

Through the 1930s and 1940s, Howland Island was home to an extensive pheasant farm operation that produced both eggs and pheasants. In 1951, a special waterfowl research project was begun to propagate duck species exotic to New York. Since 1962, the area has been managed for the natural production of waterfowl.

Hunting is allowed on portions of Howland Island, so be sure to wear colorful clothing if you venture out during May or from mid-October through November. If you encounter signs saying "Baited Area, hunting or entry within posted area prohibited," you can ignore them. Personnel from the D.E.C. clarified that hunting is prohibited in these areas, but walking and bicycling are allowed.

Trail Directions
- From Howland Island Road, ride across the bridge over the Erie Canal.
- Pass a grass trail to the right. (This will be part of your return loop.)
- At 0.7 mile, pass a trail to the right, then a grass trail to the left. Continue straight on the gravel road.
- Pass a yellow metal gate at 0.9 mile.
- Reach a "T" and turn left.
- Pass lily ponds and head uphill.
- Pass a D.E.C. building to the right, then pass an intersection.
- Climb another hill, and pass a trail to the left.

- Pass a trail to the right.
- Reach a water channel, earthen bridge, and yellow barricade. (Beyond here is the alternate parking area.)
- Turn around, and follow the gravel road back past two trail junctions.
- At the third trail, turn left on two gravel tracks.
- Pass a trail to the right.
- Bear right at a "Y."
- Pass a pond on the right.
- Ride between two ponds.
- Pass a trail on the right.
- At 3.7 miles, reach a "T" and turn right (S).
- At the next intersection, turn left off the gravel tracks, riding uphill on a grass trail.
- You'll enter a pleasant green tunnel and a long gradual downhill.
- Pass a pond.
- Reach a "Y" and bear left past a pond.
- Continue straight past a trail junction.
- Pass another pond.
- Pass a yellow metal gate.
- Reach the gravel road, and turn left to cross the Erie Canal bridge back to the parking area.

Date Enjoyed: _____

Notes:

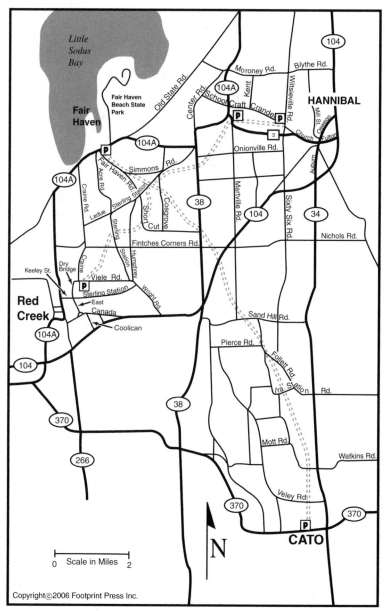

Cato-Fair Haven Trail & Hannibal-Hojack Trail

30.

Cato — Fair Haven Trail
(Cayuga County Trail)

Location: Fair Haven to Cato, Cayuga County

Parking: Southeast side of Route 104A, Fair Haven (a dirt parking area at a brown-and-yellow sign saying "Cayuga County Trail." Located behind Screwy Louie's Sport Shop. Across the street is Hadcock Sales and Guiseppe's Sub and Pizza Shop.) N43º 18.989 - W76º 42.055

Alternative Parking: Route 370, west of Cato (next to Cato Station, 2487 West Main Street). N43º 10.096 - W76º 34.552

Riding Time: 1.5 hours one way

Length: 13 miles one way

Difficulty:

Surface: Cinder, hard-packed dirt, and mowed grass

Trail Markings: Brown signs with yellow lettering "Cayuga County Trail, Fair Haven — Cato, 14 miles."
Road crossings have stop signs.

Uses:

Facilities: A portable toilet at the Route 104A end, benches along the trail. Restaurants in Fair Haven and Cato.

Dogs: OK on leash

Contact: Cayuga County Planning Board
160 Genesee Street, Auburn, NY 13021-1276
(315) 253-1276

Cayuga County Office of Tourism
131 Genesee Street, Auburn, NY 13021
(800) 499-9615
http://tourcayuga.com/

Here's a pleasant country ride to get you away from urban chaos. The trail is mainly a raised bed through woods, swamps, and Christmas tree farms. It's an easy ride, shaded by a canopy of trees. In wet weather, be ready to ride through and around some puddles. The trail starts in Fair Haven, home of the 865-acre Fair Haven Beach State Park, which has cabins and camping. Consider making this trail a weekend getaway, camping at the park and biking during the day. If it's warm, bring your swimsuits for a dip in Lake Ontario at the park's beach. Enjoy a meal at the Pleasant Beach Hotel and Restaurant overlooking Little Sodus Bay, or savor the homemade pastries at the Fly By Night Cookie Company. The Cato Hotel and Tavern on Route 370 is located just one block east of the trail.

Cato is nestled among the unique glacial ridges known as drumlins. Drumlins are long, narrow, rounded hills of sediment, formed when the glaciers scoured our countryside. These ridges sit north-south across our region and resemble an old-fashioned washboard.

This rail bed was part of the Lehigh Valley Railroad, which transported coal, passengers, and farm products from Pennsylvania to Lake Ontario. The coal was processed at a big coaling facility on Little Sodus Bay and transferred to steamships. This rail line opened in 1871. The coal dock in North Fair Haven was completed in 1872, and the first coal was dug in Athens, PA, on May 16 in 1872. Unfortunately, the rail line wasn't successful, and it closed in the early 1930s, earlier than most lines. The rails north of Cato were torn up before World War II. Cayuga County acquired the right of way and built this trail in the 1980s.

Trail Distance Between Major Roads:

Fair Haven to Sterling Station Road	1.6 miles
Sterling Station Road to Route 38	2.0 miles
Route 38 to Fintches Corners Road	0.7 mile
Fintches Corners Road to Route 104	0.3 mile
Route 104 to Sand Hill Road	2.0 miles
Sand Hill Road to Follett Road	1.2 miles
Follett Road to Ira Station Road	1.1 miles
Ira Station Road to Watkins Road	2.2 miles
Watkins Road to Route 370	1.7 miles

Trail Directions

- From the Fair Haven parking lot, head southeast toward the portable toilet to find the trail.
- Cross Simmons Road.
- Cross Sterling Station Road, and continue straight. The Hannibal — Hojack Rail Trail (Trail #31, see page 165) crosses here. This was part of the Hojack Rail System. The large yellow house nearby was the Sterling Station, which served both rail lines.
- Head uphill, and cross Cosgrove Road at 2.0 miles.
- Cross Route 38.

- Cross Fintches Corners Road. You've come 4.3 miles.
- The trail turns to mowed grass between Fintches Corners Road and Route 104. An old warehouse is on your right. The path parallels Queens Farms Road.
- Cross Route 104. Ride on a metal bridge over Sterling Creek. If you see signs saying "No Wheeled Vehicles," you can ignore them. They mean ATVs. Bicycles are allowed on this trail.
- Pass ponds on your left. This is a scenic spot to take a break.
- Cross Martville Road.
- Cross Sand Hill Road.
- Head downhill to cross a small creek. If you're lucky, cows will be grazing along the creek to your left.
- Cross Pierce Road. You've come 7.5 miles.
- Ride across a small bridge over a creek.
- Cross Follett Road. This is a short, rough section. A pond on the right is partly hidden by a line of trees along the trail.
- Cross Ira Station Road. To the right is Ira Corners, which was settled in 1805. By 1820 this town had two stores and a hotel.
- Continue past a beautiful pond/wetland on your right.
- Cross Watkins Road. You've come 11.1 miles.
- Cross Veley Road.
- The trail ends at Route 370. To your right is the first gristmill in Ira Corners, built in 1818 by John Hooker. The town of Cato is uphill to the left. It has a hardware store, grocery store, diner, pizza restaurant, gas station, and the Cato Hotel and Tavern.

Date Enjoyed: _____

Notes:

31.

Hannibal — Hojack Trail

Location:	Red Creek to Hannibal (see map on page 161), Cayuga County
Directions:	Follow Route 104A north through Red Creek. In the village, pass Viele's Agway, and turn right at the Red Creek Fire Department onto Keeley Street. Turn left at the first intersection onto Dry Bridge / Viele Road. Park along Viele Road at the trail intersection. N43º 15.812 - W76º 42.613
Alternative Parking:	Along Route 3 at the trail crossing. N43º 19.779 - W76º 37.613
Alternative Parking:	Near corner of Crandall and Wiltsieville Roads. N43º 19.725 - W76º 35.915
Riding Time:	1.5 hours one way
Length:	8.5 miles one way
Difficulty:	👣 👣
Surface:	Crushed cinder and mowed grass
Trail Markings:	Brown signs with yellow lettering "Cayuga County Trail"
Uses:	🚶 🚲 🎿 🏃
Dogs:	OK on leash
Contact:	Cayuga County Planning Board 160 Genesee Street, Auburn, NY 13021-1276 (315) 253-1276
	Cayuga County Office of Tourism 131 Genesee Street, Auburn, NY 13021 (800) 499-9615 http://tourcayuga.com/

This trail was part of the Hojack Rail System, just like the Webster, Hilton, and Hamlin sections that are all found in *Take Your Bike — Family Rides in the Rochester Area*. The area is rugged, and the trail winds around the hills and follows the creeks and streams, making it a more enjoyable ride than one that goes in a straight line to its destination. This trail is less used than the Fair Haven to Cato segment. There are no parking lots, so you have to park along the intersecting roads.

Work is proceeding to extend this rail trail west from Viele Road through Red Creek to Wolcott. A rough trail has been cleared but it is still too rough for biking. A gap exists where a bridge is out in Red Creek.

Trail Distance Between Major Roads:

Viele Road to Sterling Station Road	1.7 miles
Sterling Station Road to Route 38	3.6 miles
Route 38 to Martville Road	1.7 miles
Martville Road to Wiltsieville Road	1.5 miles

Trail Directions

- After parking along Viele Road, head NE. (Note: The trail going SE comes to a dead end within 0.5 mile.)
- Cross Fintches Corners Road.
- Cross a bridge.
- Dip down as you cross Sterling Station Road.
- Cross Humphrey Road.
- Cross Short Cut Road.
- The trail comes out onto Sterling Station Road for a short distance to skirt private property.
- At the split-rail fence bear right to regain the trail heading toward Hannibal. You'll cross the Fair Haven to Cato section of Cayuga County Trail (Trail #30). You are now riding parallel to Sterling Station Road.
- Cross Cosgrove Road. The trail veers east, away from Sterling Station Road.
- Cross a bridge.
- Cross Route 38.
- Cross another bridge.
- Cross Onionville Road.
- Cross Martville Road. Parking is available here.
- Cross another bridge.
- The trail ends at Wiltsieville Road. (Beyond this the trail continues for 0.1 mile, then it's blocked and labeled "no trespassing.")

Date Enjoyed: _____

Notes:

The Erie Canal

The idea for the Erie Canal was born in our very own Finger Lakes area — in Canandaigua to be more precise. To be absolutely accurate; the idea was born in the Canandaigua jail, which at the time was the second floor of Sheriff Elijah Tilloson's hotel. The prisoner who dared to dream this grand folly was Jesse Hawley, a once wealthy businessman, besieged with debt from his less than lucrative freight forwarding business. Hawley had attempted to make a business out of moving flour and wheat from farms in the area to the Mynderse Mill at the falls on the Seneca River (now Seneca Falls), then to market in New York City. The land and water route available to him was difficult, dangerous, and costly. Using maps in the Canandaigua jail, Hawley sketched the route for a man-made waterway, linking Lake Erie to the Hudson River. He wrote fourteen articles detailing the concept, benefits, route, and cost for an idea that many ridiculed as "the effusions of a maniac."

In 1809, a member of the Ontario County legislature took the articles to Albany for investigation. Mayor of New York City, Dewitt Clinton, took up the cause. The canal became his political passion as he became Governor of New York. Ground was broken for the Erie Canal in 1817. Eight years later, the canal opened. American ingenuity overcame a multitude of obstacles along the way. America had no engineers or engineering schools in the early 1800s. Clinton asked a British engineer to head this project, but he declined the offer, forcing Clinton to use American leadership. The closest America had were lawyers who had some surveying experience. The canal became a huge on-the-job-training endeavor. It led to the development of Rensselaer Polytechnic Institute in Troy, the Civil Engineering Department of Union College, and Rochester Institute of Technology.

These inexperienced engineers had to devise ways to build locks, including ones to overcome the 60-foot rise of the Niagara Escarpment in Lockport. They had to develop waterproof cement, blast through bedrock, and build aqueducts, including the 804-foot long span over the Genesee River in downtown Rochester and the 1-mile span over the Irondequoit Valley in Pittsford. A challenge for the western end of the canal was how to keep enough water in the canal, especially during summer droughts. To accomplish this, feeders were built, rerouting water from lakes, streams, and reservoirs along the way into the canal.

Clinton's Folly, the original Erie Canal, was only 40 feet wide and 4 feet deep. However, it was an instant economic success. It shortened the transportation of goods between Buffalo and New York City from 6 weeks to 10 days and lowered the cost of transporting one ton of freight from $100 to $10. All of a sudden goods could move east to market and immigrants could move west to open land. Business boomed.

By 1835, the canal was log jammed with too much traffic. Thus, a major effort was undertaken to enlarge the Erie Canal. Locks were doubled to allow two-way traffic and lengthened to accommodate longer boats. The canal was straightened in various places to decrease its total length and it was widened to 70 feet and deepened to 7 feet. This second version of the Erie Canal is now known as the Enlarged Erie Canal.

Over the years, additional work was done. In some areas, there was a second Enlarged Erie Canal. The next major change came in 1918. The canal was once again over capacity. By now, technological know-how had improved. Engineers now knew how to incorporate the canal into existing rivers and control the water levels. The Erie Canal was once again enlarged and moved. This time it took over riverbeds such as the Clyde River and the Mohawk River. The new and improved version was renamed the Barge Canal. The name reverted back to the historic one (Erie Canal) when commercial traffic dwindled in the mid 1900s.

In sections, for example, Lockport to Greece and Fairport to Palmyra, there is little difference in location of the three canals. With each enhancement, the ditch simply got larger. In other places, the three waterways had distinctly different locations, and all three can be seen today. The stretch from Port Byron through Jordan to Camillus is an example of the latter.

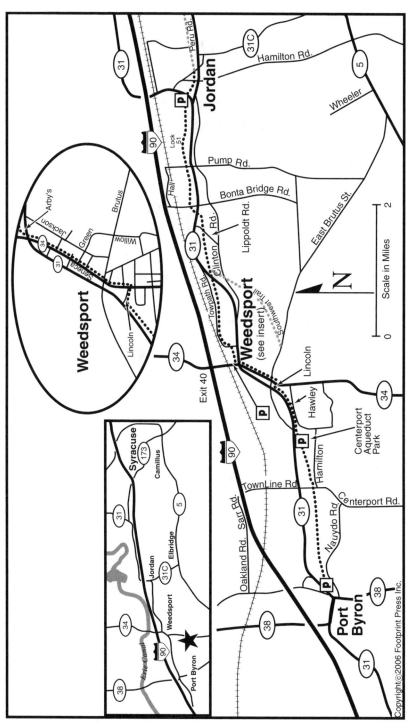

Erie Canalway Trail (Port Byron to Jordan)

32.

Erie Canalway Trail
(Port Byron to Jordan)

Location: Port Byron, Weedsport, and Jordan (south of the N.Y.S. Thruway), Cayuga and Onondaga Counties

Directions: From Port Byron, head east on Route 31. Park in the canal bed at Randolph J. Schasel Village Park on the south side of Route 31. A small brown-and-yellow sign, "Cayuga County Erie Canal Trail" is visible from Route 31.   N43º 2.241 - W76º 37.194

Alternative Parking: Centerport Aqueduct Park, Route 31, between Port Byron and Weedsport.   N43º 2.600 - W76º 34.540

Alternative Parking: Behind the Arby's at the corner of Route 34 and Route 31 in Weedsport.   N43º 02.948 - W76º 33.841

Alternative Parking: North Main Street, Jordan, in front of Jordan Aqueduct Garden.   N43º 04.002 - W76º 28.932

Riding Time: 2 hours one way

Length: 9.3 miles one way

Difficulty: 👣 👣

Surface: Dirt, gravel, and grass trail

Trail Markings: Some signs, "Cayuga County Erie Canal Trail"

Uses: 🚶 🚲 🎿 🏃

Dogs: OK

Contact: County Planner
Cayuga County Planning Board
160 Genesee Street, Auburn, NY 13021-1276
(315) 253-1276

Cayuga County Parks and Trails Commission
East Lake Road, Auburn, N.Y. 13021
(315) 253-5611
http://co.cayuga.ny.us/parks/index.html

This trail follows the towpath or the location of the former towpath from a previous version of the Erie Canal (called the Enlarged Erie Canal), not the current Erie Canal. For a short history of the Erie Canal, refer to page 167.

The 1.5-mile section of Enlarged Erie Canal that remains between Port Byron and Centerport was made accessible to the public in the Fall of 1987. The Lock 52 Historical Society and concerned community members cleared the former towpath and canal bed to make the canal with its hand-placed stone sides visible.

The Randolph J. Schasel Village Park in Port Byron marks the beginning of this trail, which is built partly in the old canal bed and includes a pavilion, playground, and basketball court. Past Centerport, the trail becomes pretty rough. The trail bed includes gravel, mowed grass, weeds, and some roads. It continues through Weedsport to Jordan. The trail actually continues another 14.8 miles through Erie Canal Park in Camillus (see Trails #33 and #34).

Weedsport derived its name from the Weed brothers, Edward and Elihu, who dug and founded Weed's Basin, a re-supply point on the original Erie Canal.

Trail Directions
- From the parking area in Randolph J. Schasel Village Park, head east on the trail between Route 31 and the basketball court. The Enlarged Erie Canal will be on your right. Further to the right is the original Erie Canal, also called Clinton's Ditch.
- At 0.9 mile, pass the Harring Brook receiver. All the water from this creek dumped into the canal.
- Cross Centerport Road.
- Cross a wooden bridge. Centerport Aqueduct will be on the right. It was built in 1835 to carry the canal over Cold Spring Brook. There is a rare dam in the creek next to the aqueduct.
- At 2.4 miles, reach Centerport Aqueduct Park and Route 31. (Parking is available here.)
- The gravel trail turns to grass and runs parallel to Route 31.
- Cross Hawley Road.
- Turn right onto the sidewalk on Lincoln Road.
- Take the next left and follow the sidewalk of Seneca Street.
- Cross Route 31 to Arby's. The trail continues behind Arby's.
- Pass the brown sign for "Cayuga County Erie Canal Trail."
- Cross a wooden bridge over Putnum Brook, then pass a pond and pen, home to ducks, geese, turkeys, and chickens.
- At 4.1 miles, reach Towpath Road, and turn left.

- Follow Towpath Road for 0.4 mile. The trail begins again on the right, after a chained gate, into the back of Cayuga County Fairgrounds. There are no signs and no parking area, simply a mowed grass path, heading southeast.
- Turn right onto the trail. You will be in a pleasant "woods tunnel" with the old canal to your left and a creek to your right.
- At 5.6 miles, cross Route 31 and bear left. (The trail to the right is the Southwest Trail that leads 2.7 miles to Weedsport High School).
- The trail will get rough. Watch carefully for woodchuck holes.
- Cross Lippoldt Road.
- At 6.5 miles, cross Route 31 again.
- Cross Bonta Bridge Road. The trail bed will improve.
- Cross Pump Road. The Enlarged Erie Canal is again on your right.
- Pass a double lock (Lock 51) from the Enlarged Erie Canal on your right.
- Cross a farm lane. The trail turns from gravel to dirt with roots.
- At 8.7 miles, cross Route 31. The trail continues in the woods behind a sign, "Jordan-Elbridge Area Church Board."
- Cross through a mowed field.
- Cross Werner Way then cross the grass behind the fire hall.
- Cross Hamilton Road.
- Immediately in front of you will be a park. Cross the park on the mowed grass inside the old canal bed until you reach North Main Street, Jordan. (Parking is available along North Main Street.) You've come 9.3 miles. [Continue straight on the gravel path between the Jordan Aqueduct Garden and the Masonic Lodge to connect with the Erie Canalway Trail #33 (Jordan to Camillus), for a 20-mile ride one way.]

Date Enjoyed: _____

Notes:

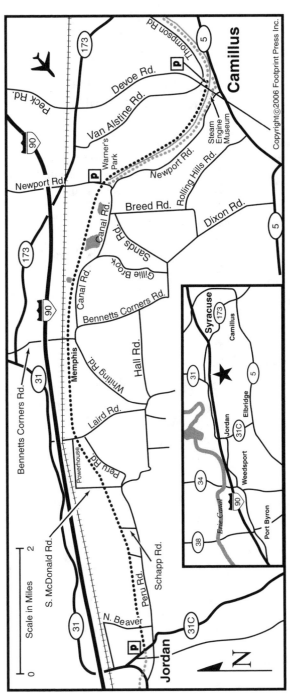

Erie Canalway Trail (Jordan to Camillus)

33.

Erie Canalway Trail
(Jordan to Camillus)

Location:	Jordan to Camillus, Onondaga County
Directions:	Park along North Main Street (Route 31C), Jordan, in front of Jordan Aqueduct Garden (between the Laundromat and Masonic Lodge).

N43° 03.949 - W76° 28.373

Alternative Parking: Warners Park, Newport Road.

N43° 04.597 - W76° 19.663

Alternative Parking: Camillus Erie Canal Park, Devoe Road.

N43° 3.149 - W76° 18.202

Riding Time:	2.5 hours one way
Length:	10.8 miles one way
Difficulty:	
Surface:	Dirt and gravel trail
Trail Markings:	None
Uses:	
Dogs:	OK
Contact:	P.O. Box 397
	Jordan, NY 13080
	(315) 689-3278

Also called the Erie Canal Parkway, this is an easy-to-follow, well-maintained trail along the abandoned Enlarged Erie Canal. For a short history of the Erie Canal, refer to page 167.

Trail Directions

- Head east along the path between Jordan Aqueduct Garden and the Masonic Lodge.
- Cross North Beaver Street as you ride through Old Erie Place Park. Picnic tables and parking are available here.
- The Enlarged Erie Canal will appear on your right.
- Pass a road on the right.
- Pass Schapp Road.

In Jordan, the former canal bed is now a beautiful park.

- Reach the waste weir on the left. This is where water from Carpenter Brook was used to help control the level of water in the Erie Canal.
- Cross South McDonald Road in Peru.
- Pass a private house and the McIntyre, a former hotel along the canal, as you approach Laird Road. You've come 4.2 miles.
- At 5.8 miles, cross Bennetts Corners Road at the town of Memphis.
- Cross under power lines.
- Pass a gravel road to the right. The trail becomes a gravel and paved roadway.
- At 8.6 miles, cross Newport Road. Across the road, enter Warners Park. (Parking is available here.)
- Pass the Camillus Sportsman's Club.
- Cross Devoe Road into Camillus Erie Canal Park. (Parking is available here.) You've come 10.8 miles.

[Continue to Trail #34 for an additional 8.5 mile loop.]

Date Enjoyed: _____

Notes:

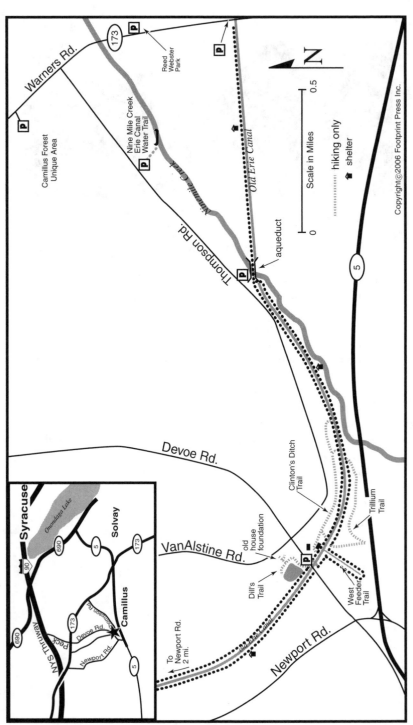

Erie Canal Park

34.

Erie Canal Park

Location: Camillus (west of Syracuse), Onondaga County
Directions: From Route 5, turn north on Devoe Road. Erie Canal Park is on the right, just south of Thompson Road. N43º 3.149 - W76º 18.202
Alternative Parking: Warners Park on Newport Road. N43º 04.597 - W76º 19.663
Alternative Parking: Reed Webster Park on Warners Road. N43º 04.111 - W76º 16.286
Alternative Parking: A pull-off at the west end of the trail on Warners Road. N43º 03.825 - W76º 16.117
Alternative Parking: A parking area off Thompson Road, near the dock and aqueduct. N43º 4.351 - W76º 16.820
Riding Time: 1.75 hour loop
Length: 8.5-mile loop
Difficulty:

Surface: Dirt and gravel trail
Trail Markings: None
Uses:

Dogs: OK on leash
Contacts: Erie Canal Park
5750 Devoe Road, Camillus, NY 13031
(315) 488-3409 www.eriecanalcamillus.com

The Enlarged Erie Canal was abandoned in 1922. (See page 167 for a short history of the Erie Canal.) It sat idle until 1972, when the Town of Camillus purchased a seven-mile stretch. Since then an army of volunteers has been busy clearing the land, building dams, refilling the canal with water, and building a replica of Sims' store. The original Sims' store was built in 1856 at the intersection of Warners Road and the canal. It served as a general store, home for the Sims family, and as a departure point for persons boarding the canal boats. The store was destroyed by fire in 1863, but the replica lives on today. The first floor is set up like the original store. The second floor houses exhibits and antiques of the era along with models of locks, aqueducts, and canal boats. Sims' Museum is open on

The Nine Mile Creek Aqueduct towpath
is now part of the Erie Canal Park Trail.

Saturdays from 9:00 AM until 1:00 PM year-round and on Sundays from 1:00 until 5:00 PM, May through October, and 1:00 until 4:00 PM, November through April.

The trails are available year-round during daylight hours. This trail circumnavigates the historic Enlarged Erie Canal and passes sections of the original Erie Canal, also called Clinton's Ditch. Rain shelters are built at several locations along the trail. It's an easy bicycle loop, perfect for family outings.

The volunteers of Town of Camillus Erie Canal Park & Sims' Store Museum plan to reconstruct the aqueduct, and to complete the trail along the south side of the canal from the aqueduct to Warners Road (Route 173). This renovation will enable riders to continue on the south side of the canal past the aqueduct, cross over at Warners Road, and return on the north side of the canal for a nice loop.

Trail Directions
- From the parking area at Sims' Store, ride west across Devoe Road, following the northeast side of the Enlarged Erie Canal. The path is paved for 0.7 mile.
- Pass a barricade, and continue straight on a dirt path.

- At 2.1 miles, before a gate to Warners Park, turn left then left again to return on the opposite side of the canal.
- Pass a sign showing where the Enlarged Erie Canal crossed Clinton's Ditch.
- At 4.2 miles, cross Devoe Road and continue straight.
- At the pedestrian bridge turn right on the West Feeder Trail.
- Reach the end of the feeder, and turn left around its end to return on the opposite side.
- Reach the canal, and turn right.
- Pass the entrance to Trillium Trail (hikers only).
- Pass the exit of Trillium Trail.
- Reach the dock at 5.6 miles. (Straight ahead leads to a dead end at the aqueduct. A parking area is to the left on Thompson Road.) Turn left, then turn right immediately to continue riding on the other side of the canal, still heading east.
- Cross the towpath next to the aqueduct that once carried canal waters over Nine Mile Creek. All that remains are the stone supports for the wooden trough.
- Reach Warners Road (Route 173) at 6.6 miles. (Parking is available across the street in Reed Webster Park.)
- Turn around and retrace your path back past the aqueduct.
- Continue straight past the dock and parking area on Thompson Road.
- Pass the culvert, which carried runoff water under the canal to Nine Mile Creek.

A portion of the Enlarged Erie Canal wall
is visible in Erie Canal Park.

•Return to the parking area at Sims' Museum.

Date Enjoyed: _____

Notes:

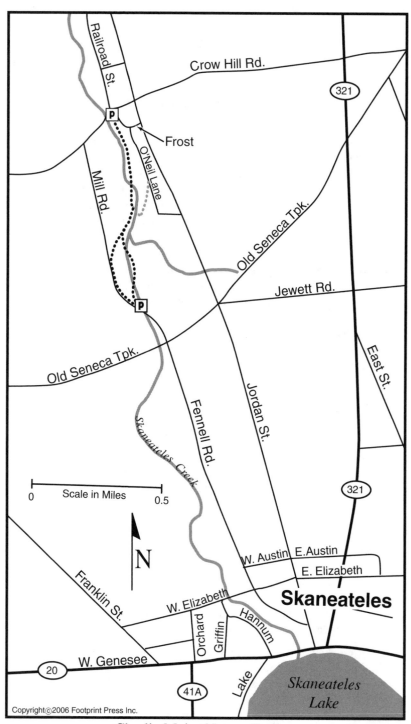

Charlie Major Nature Trail

35.

Charlie Major Nature Trail

Location:	North of the village of Skaneateles, Onondaga County
Directions:	From Route 20 in Skaneateles, turn north onto Jordan Street, then left onto Fennell Road. Fennell will turn into Mill Road. Look for a gravel parking area, 500 feet north of Old Seneca Turnpike, on the east side of Mill Road. A gray sign with black lettering "Nature Trail" marks the area.
	N42º 57.777 - W76º 26.464

Alternative Parking: A parking area on Crow Hill Road near the corner of Railroad Street and Skaneateles Creek, marked with a wooden "Charlie Major Nature Trail" sign.

N42º 58.386 - W76º 26.640

Riding Time:	20 minute loop
Length:	1.6-mile loop
Difficulty:	👣
Surface:	Dirt and crushed stone trail
Trail Markings:	None
Uses:	🚶 🚴 ⛷ 🏃 🏂 ♿
Dogs:	OK on leash
Contact:	Town of Skaneateles Recreation Department
	24 Jordan Street, Skaneateles, NY 13152
	(315) 685-3473 or (315) 685-5607

The Charlie Major Nature Trail was named after Charles T. Major, Jr., a public figure who featured prominently in the history and development of this rail trail. Mr. Major served as village justice, town justice, town board member, and town supervisor from the 1950s through the 1990s, often taking town employees on nature walks to this obscure place that had featured prominently in the area's history. The nature trail was his idea. Today he is a state supreme court justice.

The early settlers, arriving in the area beginning in 1794, recognized that the drop of 100 feet in the flow of water down the Skaneateles Outlet from Skaneateles Lake north, would furnish water power for industry. This cheap source of waterpower gave rise to the bustling community of Mottville. A railroad for horse-drawn cars was built along the creek in 1840, followed by a plank road which was used only a few years. Then, the steam railroad came in 1866. Sawmills, gristmills, tanneries, woolen mills, distilleries, and paper mills dotted the waterfront. As these industries declined, the factories became the sites for the manufacture of vacuum cleaners, cement blocks, tiles, chemicals, and medical instruments.

Remains of this industrial era can be seen along the trail today, identified by numbered sign posts. To the left of Point #1 are parts of the dam and headrace from Mottville Woodworking Factory. This factory was built in 1807 and became a woodworking factory that made tools for farmers by 1816. Across the creek are stone ruins from Mottville Woolen Factory, built in 1830 to produce fine cashmeres and woolens. In 1862 it was renamed Morton's Shawl Mill after the new owner Thomas Morton. It closed in 1890. Another nearby site had a sawmill, gristmill, and distillery dating from 1800. In 1852 Morton's Woolen Mill was built on the site, primarily to make uniforms for Union soldiers. The mill closed in 1890, and burned in 1894. Also nearby was Mottville Flour Mill, a three-story building capable of grinding 500 bushels a day. Part of the building was used as the railroad station.

Point #2 identifies the original site of saw and grist mills. In 1857 the Earll, Tallman Distillery was built to produce cologne and alcohol. In 1882 the distillery was converted to a paper mill and became known as Lakeside Paper Company. This paper mill (the Little Mill) was connected by a railroad to the Big Mill (see below) and concrete supports that once supported huge steam pipes between the mills still stand in the creek.

Point #3 identifies the dam that once created the mill pond for Lakeside Paper Mill. Point #4 is the old Skaneateles Paper Company which had a long lineage beginning as a saw mill, then a grist mill, then a distillery before becoming a paper mill. The paper mill burned and was rebuilt several times, eventually being called "the Big Mill." Over the succeeding years, the Big Mill was put to use by many companies, including a construction company, a boat company, a tile manufacturer, a vacuum cleaner manufacturer, a cement block maker, and even a ceramics manufacturer.

Point #5 identifies the dam and mill pond from the Skaneateles Paper Company. Finally, Point #6 is an area called Willow Glen, although it's uncertain how it got this name. It's the site of the first power dam on the outlet, erected in 1794. Then, like other areas on the outlet, the site saw a succession of uses from saw mill, to grist mill, to shoemaker's shop. Willow Glen is said to have had the first school house in the area, and the first distillery. Robert Earll, who factored heavily in the area's early history held church services in his house here.

When the city of Syracuse began using the water from Skaneateles Lake for its drinking water, it took over control of the dam at the outlet. The water level in the creek was lowered below a level necessary for mill operations, so other methods of power generation had to be sought. At one point, so little water flowed down the Skaneateles Outlet that the sewage concentration became high enough to initiate an outbreak of typhoid. A second epidemic swept the area in the 1920s, when well water became contaminated. Charles Major, Senior, was responsible for organizing a town committee to bring piped water to the community.

The rail line, eventually known as the Short Line, helped to maintain prosperity in the community by serving the industries along the outlet. It also carried passengers from the New York Central Railroad at Skaneateles Junction to Skaneateles where they could board the steamboats for trips around the lake. Today, the rails are gone and a serene path follows Skaneateles Creek for part of its journey, as it flows northward from Skaneateles Lake into the Seneca River. The trail is equally pleasant as a walk or a bike ride. Go when the leaves are off the trees to get the best views of the old mill and factory ruins.

Trail Directions
•From the parking area on Mill Road, head northwest on the trail.
•Cross a wooden bridge over Skaneateles Creek.
•The creek will now be on your left, parallel to the trail.
•Cross a second bridge.
•At 0.3 mile, reach a "Y" intersection. (The trail to the left goes for 0.12 mile to Mill Road.) Continue straight (S).
•Immediately after a brick shed is a trail to the right. Notice the dam in the creek to the right. (The trail to the right heads uphill for 0.13 mile to O'Neil Lane, past the dam, and crosses the old mill race of Mottville Woodworking Factory.) Continue straight.
•At 0.5 mile, cross a bridge over the creek.
•Reach Crow Hill Road at 0.8 mile. Turn around and ride back on the same path.
•When the trail comes to a "Y," bear right.
•Turn left onto Mill Road, and ride the road back to the parking area.

Date Enjoyed: _____

Notes:

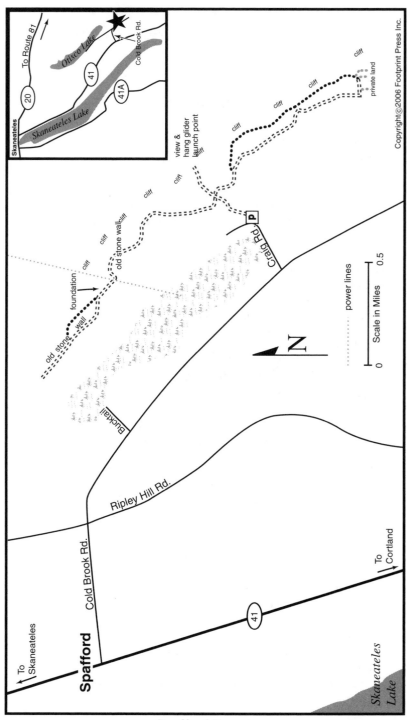

Spafford Forest

36.

Spafford Forest

Location:	Spafford, Onondaga County
Directions:	From Route 41 along the southeast shore of Skaneateles Lake, turn east onto Cold Brook Road. Pass Ripley Hill Road and Bucktail, then turn left onto Craig Road. Park in the grass parking area labeled by a brown and yellow "Spafford Forest" sign. N42o 47.533 - W76o 13.268
Riding Time:	1 hour loop
Length:	6.2-mile loop
Difficulty:	🥾 🥾 🥾
Surface:	A combination of dirt jeep roads, grassy double-track, fire lanes, and woodland paths.
Trail Markings:	None
Uses:	
Dogs:	OK on leash
Contact:	Highland Forest/Spafford Forest Box 31, Highland Park Road, Fabius, NY 13063 (315) 683-5550 www.onondagacountyparks.com

The hardest part of this ride is the climb from the parking area to Spafford Ridge. Once you're up, the trails are mild and easy to ride, following the rolling terrain at the top of the ridge. Northeast of the trails is a steep cliff. The trail straight back from the parking lot leads to a hang glider launch point with a great view.

There is a confusing jumble of trails that lead to private property at the south end. It's best to take a compass with you, so you can be sure to select a trail that returns northwest. Also, watch for a cliff to your right as a gauge that you're returning northwest.

Trail Directions
•From the parking area, head uphill on the dirt trail.
•At the trail junction on top of the ridge, turn left.
•Pass an old stone wall, powerlines, then an old foundation.

An easy double-track trail awaits once you climb
to the ridge in Spafford Forrest.

- When the grassy double-track trail splits, bear right.
- Bear right again at the next junction.
- When the trail ends, turn around and ride straight back to the main trail junction.
- Turn left and ride to the hang glider launch point. This makes a nice break spot.
- Return to the main trail junction, and turn left onto the dirt jeep road.
- Pass a woods path on your left. It will be your return leg.
- At the southernmost part of the trail network, you'll encounter a bewildering array of trails. Choose the left option each time to swing back into Spafford Forest and stay off private property.
- Watch for the cliff to your right as you return on the woods path.
- When it meets the dirt jeep road, turn right.
- At the main trail junction, turn left to head downhill to the parking area.

Date Enjoyed: _____

Notes:

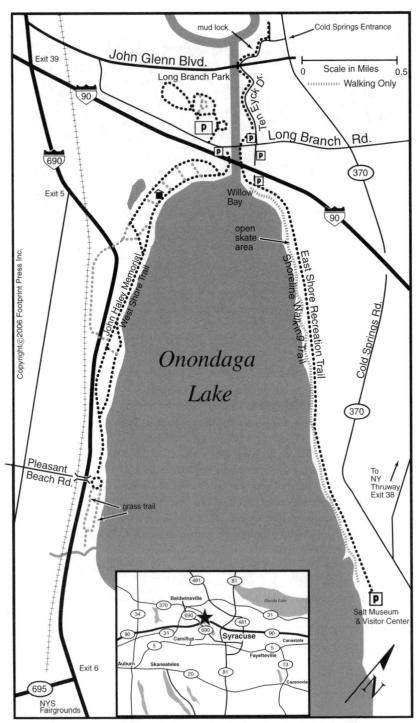

Onondaga Lake Park Trails

37.

Onondaga Lake Park Trails
(West Shore Trail, East Shore Trail, Long Branch Park)

Location:	Onondaga Lake shoreline, Liverpool, Onondaga County
Directions:	From I-90, take Liverpool exit 38. Head north on Route 57 (Oswego Street), then left (W) on Route 35 (Long Branch Road.) Cross the bridge over Onondaga Lake Outlet, and park in lots on either side. N43º 07.101 - W76º 14.632 (N of Long Branch Rd.)
Alternative Parking:	At Long Branch Park. N43º 07.005 - W76º 14.958
Riding Time:	2 hours total loop
Length:	12.5 miles total loop
Difficulty:	

Surface:	Paved trails and park roads, stone dust trails in Long Branch Park
Trail Markings:	Some trail signs
Uses:	
Amenities:	Restrooms at Willow Bay, portable toilet at Long Branch. Bike and in-line skate rentals are available at Willow Bay.
Dogs:	OK on leash
Contact:	Onondaga Lake Park
	PO Box 146, Liverpool, NY 13088
	(315) 453-6712 www.co.onondaga.ny.us

From the cluster of parking areas at the north end of Onondaga Lake you can choose among several riding options or combine them all for a full 12.5 mile ride. This is a busy trail network, especially in summer. The trails are mainly flat and easy, but your biggest challenge will be dodging in-line skaters. Of course, you won't find skaters on the stone dust trails in Long Branch Park, and they'll be fewer in numbers on the West Shore Trail.

Ten Eyck Drive

Riding Time:	20 minutes round trip
Length:	2 miles round trip

This is a paved road where cars are allowed (one-way, south only) but they go slowly, so you can safely ride. You'll pass remains of Mud Lock, which allowed passage from Onondaga Lake to the Oswego Canal and was the site of a lively tavern. Mud Lock was originally Oswego Canal Lock 5, built in 1828 with wood. Eight years later it was upgraded to stone. Its nickname, Mud Lock, came from the fact that it was built in "mud" quicksand. Near this is the Wegmans Good Dog Park. Ten Eyck Drive dead-ends where the Onondaga Lake Outlet meets the Seneca River.

Long Branch Park
Riding Time: 15 minute loop
Length: 1.5-mile loop

This was the site of an early 20th century resort. Today, eight-feet-wide stone dust trails wind through woods, passing pavilions, rest rooms and picnic tables. The gentle hills are easy to ride. Enjoy the 1.5-mile outer loop.

East Shore Recreation Trail
Riding Time: 45 minutes round trip
Length: 5 miles round trip

The Onondaga Lake East Shore Trail has separate
biking and walking trails.

From Long Branch Road, head south on the 20-feet-wide, paved East Shore Recreation trail for 2.5 miles to the Salt Museum and Visitor Center. This is a busy trail. Your companions on this trail will be other bikers, in-line skaters, a tram, and walkers during non-prime hours. Parallel to this trail is the paved hiking-only Shoreline Walking Trail.

John Haley Memorial West Shore Trail
Riding Time: 35 minute loop
Length: 4-mile loop

This trail is used less than the East Shore Trail. Head south from the west side of Onondaga Lake Outlet. Bear left on the paved trail at each junction to stay close to the lake on the outbound leg. For the return leg, again bear left to follow the stone dust side loops.

The Onondaga Lake West Shore Recreation Trail is now paved.

Date Enjoyed: _____
Notes:

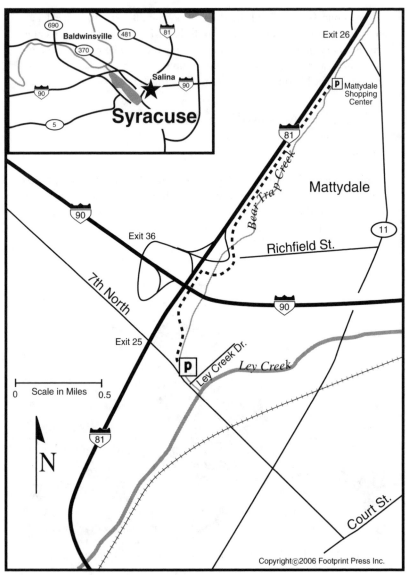

Bear Trap Creek Bikeway

38.

Bear Trap Creek Bikeway

Location: Town of Salina, Onondaga County

Directions: From Route 81 take exit 25 and head south on 7th North. Turn left onto Ley Creek Drive and left into a parking lot. N43º 05.235 - W76º 09.858

Alternative Parking: Behind K-Mart at Mattydale Shopping Center (on Route 11 at the corner of I-81). N43º 06.376 - W76º 09.024

Riding Time: 30 minutes

Length: 3 miles round trip

Difficulty:

Surface: Paved trail

Trail Markings: None

Uses:

Dogs: OK on leash

Contact: Town of Salina
(315) 451-8110

Onondaga County Parks
PO Box 146, Liverpool, NY 13088
(315) 453-6712   www.onondagacountyparks.com

This 8-foot-wide paved trail was built during the Route 81 improvements in the 1980s. Running between Bear Trap Creek and busy I-81, it can get noisy, but offers a nice paved trail, free from cars. Wear sunscreen.

Trail Directions

- From the Ley Creek Drive parking area, head north on the paved trail.
- When you reach Mattydale Shopping Center, turn around and bike back south.

Date Enjoyed: _____

Notes:

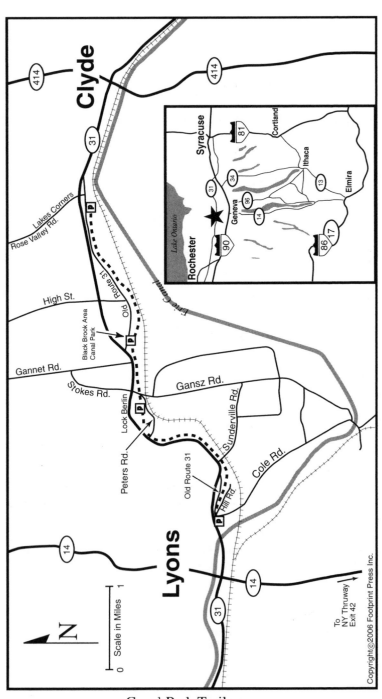

Canal Park Trailway

39.

Canal Park Trailway

Location:	Lyons to Clyde, Wayne County
Parking:	Heading east on Route 31 through Lyons, cross over the Erie Canal, then turn right onto Cole Road. Quickly turn left onto Hill Road, and park along the road near this intersection. N43º 03.671 - W76º 58.556
Alternative Parking:	Lock Berlin Park on Peters Road. N43º 04.566 - W76º 56.969
Alternative Parking:	Black Brook Area Canal Park on Old Route 31. N43º 04.748 - W76º 56.188
Alternative Parking:	Roadside at the end of the trail, near 9928 Old Route 31. N43º 5.317 - W76º 54.086
Riding Time:	1 hour one way
Length:	5.1 miles one way
Difficulty:	👣 👣 👣
Surface:	Mowed-grass path
Trail Markings:	2 by 3-foot, white, blue, and faded red signs
Uses:	
Facilities:	Black Brook Area Canal Park has picnic pavilions, restrooms, and a playground; Lock Berlin has picnic tables.
Dogs:	OK on leash
Contact:	Wayne County Planning Department 9 Pearl Street, Lyons, NY 14489 (315) 946-5919

Follow history back in time as you pedal from the existing Erie Canal to the original Clinton's Ditch of 1817 and the Enlarged Erie Canal of the 1850s. Along the way pass stone locks, long abandoned. On one trip we saw wild turkey and a beaver repairing his den. Locals say the old canal waters are a great fishing spot for bass and sunfish.

The Erie Canal, dubiously called "Clinton's Ditch," opened for operation in 1825. It was a 40-foot-wide water channel with locks 90 feet long and 15 feet wide. Boats with loads up to 75 tons could navigate the waters.

By 1840 a greater capacity was needed as commerce along the canal boomed, and the canal was enlarged to 70 feet wide. Locks increased to 110 feet long and 18 feet wide allowing cargos up to 200 tons.

By 1909, the canal was overcapacity again. This time the canal was rerouted in places as it was enlarged. The name was changed to reflect its growing purpose. The new-and-improved Barge Canal opened in 1918 allowing cargos of 3,000 tons to pass through its 45-foot-wide locks. The opening of the Saint Lawrence Seaway eliminated the need to transfer goods to barges and rendered the the canal obsolete. The name was changed back to its historic one: the Erie Canal.

You can zip to and from this adventure on the New York State Thruway, but why not slow down and follow Route 96 for at least one leg of the journey. You'll be rewarded with a tour through stately old towns and spectacular examples of cobblestone houses along the way. (For more information on unique local cobblestone buildings, pick up a copy of *Cobblestone Quest — Road Tours of New York's Historic Buildings*.)

Avoid riding here in spring when the trail can be wet and soft. The hills are mild, but beware of woodchuck holes. The trail used to extend another 0.7-mile west to Route 14, but that section is no longer maintained.

Trail Distance Between Major Roads:

Hill Road to Sunderville Road	0.7 mile
Sunderville Road to Peters Road	1.0 mile
Peters Road to Gansz Road	0.6 mile
Gansz Road to Black Brook Area Canal Park	0.7 mile
Black Brook Area Canal Park to Route 31	2.1 miles

Trail Directions
• From the intersection of Cole Road and Hill Road, follow the grass path between Old Route 31 and Hill Road.
• Pass an old stone bridge abutment. Clinton's Ditch is on your left.
• The trail passes through a low area that can be muddy in wet weather and may not get mowed regularly.
• Cross Sunderville Road. Clinton's Ditch continues to be on your left.
• Pass two dirt dikes across the old canal bed.
• Cross Peters Road.
• Notice the large beaver dam across the old canal bed.
• Pass an abandoned, stone, double lock. A park is at the lock (Lock Berlin) with picnic tables and grills.

- Cross Gansz Road. The canal is dammed here and becomes a trickle in a ditch from here east.
- Cross a small wooden bridge.
- A short side trail to the left leads to stonework around a feeder creek, which is actually half of an original Clinton's Ditch lock rebuilt to form a waste weir.
- A path to the left, across a crooked wooden bridge, leads to Black Brook Area Canal Park. This park has restrooms, a pavilion, picnic tables, grills, and a playground.
- The mowed path ends at a driveway. You can turn around here to head back or turn left onto the driveway (9928 Old Route 31), then right (E) onto Old Route 31, and ride 0.9 mile to the junction of Route 31 where parking is available.

Date Enjoyed: _____

Notes:

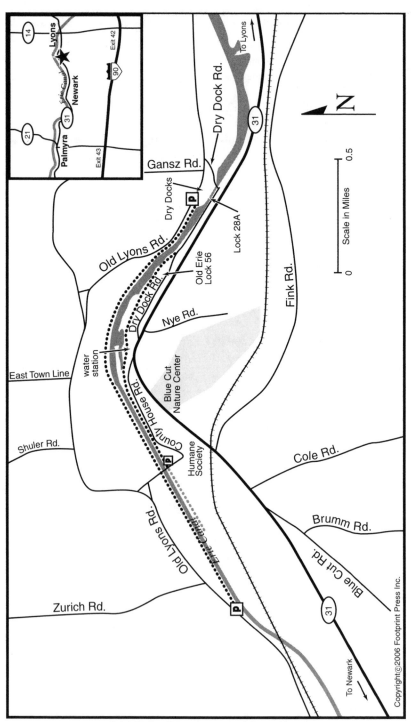

Old Erie Canal Lock 56 Trail

40.

Old Erie Canal Lock 56 Trail

Location: Lyons, Wayne County
Parking: From Route 31, west of Lyons, turn north onto Dry Dock Road. Cross over the Erie Canal and turn left onto Old Lyons Road. Park on the left, just past Lock 28A and the dry dock area.
N43º 03.811 - W77º 01.243

Alternative Parking: An unmarked dirt parking loop off Old Lyons Road, west of the County House Road intersection.
N43º 03.965 - W77º 03.313

Alternative Parking: Southeast of the County House Road bridge over the Erie Canal. N43º 03.926 - W77º 02.600

Riding Time: 45 minute loop
Length: 4.5-mile loop
Difficulty:

Surface: Mowed-grass trail
Trail Markings: None
Uses:

Dogs: Pets OK on leash
Contact: NYS Canal Corp.
PO Box 189, Albany, NY 12201-0189
1-800-422-6254   www.canals.state.ny.us

This is an historical tour of the Erie Canal, beginning at Lock 28A, an operational lock on the Erie Canal and home of the canal's dry dock. A dry dock is a siding where boats can float in. When the water is drained out, the boats sit high and dry on scaffolding for winter storage or repairs. This dry dock is the winter home of two canal tour boats: The Colonial Belle that operates out of Fairport and the Amita II that operates out of Syracuse.

On the opposite side of the canal, you'll pass Lock 56, a remnant from the smaller Enlarged Erie Canal. Refer to page 167 for a short history of the Erie Canal. This trail is part of the Erie Canalway Trail that will some day span from Buffalo to Albany.

Colonial Belle, a tour boat out of Fairport,
sits in winter dry dock.

Trail Directions
- From the parking area near Lock 28A, head west on the mowed-grass path, away from the lock.
- Keep the Erie Canal to your left and pass County House Road.
- When the trail ends at a parking loop on Old Lyons Road, turn around and return to the County House Road bridge.
- This time turn right and cross the Erie Canal on the County House Road bridge.
- Over the bridge, turn left onto the mowed-grass path. The Erie Canal is again to your left.
- Pass a water pumping station.
- Continuing east, the Enlarged Erie Canal will be to your right.
- Pass Old Erie Canal Lock 56.
- When the trail dead ends at Dry Dock Road, follow the road left over the Erie Canal.
- Turn left onto Old Lyons Road to pass Lock 28A and the dry dock to return to your car.

Enlarged Erie Canal Lock 56 now sits parallel to the
current Erie Canal, near operational Lock 28A.

Date Enjoyed: _____
Notes:

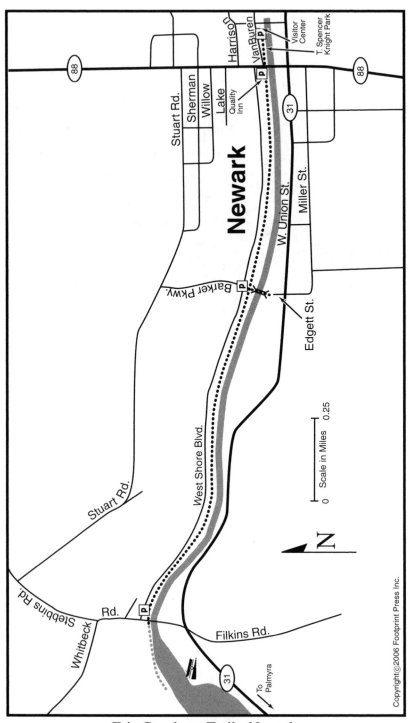

Erie Canalway Trail - Newark

41.

Erie Canalway Trail — Newark

Location:	Newark, Wayne County
Parking:	From Route 31, west of Newark, turn north onto Whitbeck Road. Cross over the Erie Canal, and turn right onto West Shore Boulevard. The parking area is immediately on the right. N43º 03.160 - W77º 07.625

Alternative Parking: A parking area off West Shore Boulevard, at the end of Barker Parkway. N43º 02.894 - W77º 06.485

Alternative Parking: At the Quality Inn on Route 88 on the north shore of the canal. N43º 02.865 - W77º 05.719

Alternative Parking: Parking slots along VanBuren Street, in front of the Visitor Center. VanBuren Street is one-way heading east. N43º 02.877- W77º 05.581

Riding Time:	35 minutes round trip
Length:	4.2 miles round trip
Difficulty:	👣 👣 👣
Surface:	Stone dust
Trail Markings:	None
Uses:	🚶 🚴 🎿 🏃 ♿
Dogs:	Pets OK on leash
Contact:	NYS Canal Corp. PO Box 189, Albany, NY 12201-0189 1-800-422-6254 www.canals.state.ny.us

This trail is part of the Erie Canalway Trail that will some day span from Buffalo to Albany. You'll find an easy ride on hard-packed stone dust, through mildly rolling hills, with views of the Erie Canal to the south. At the east end, in Newark, is the T. Spencer Knight Park - a fine spot for a picnic.

Trail Directions
• From the parking area near Whitbeck Road, head left (E) on the trail. (The trail to the west dead-ends shortly, but will eventually be connected to the Erie Canalway Trail in Palmyra.)

- In 1.0 mile, pass the parking area near Barker Parkway and a pedestrian bridge over the canal to the right to Edgett Street.
- In another 0.7 mile, pass the Quality Inn.
- The trail continues under Route 88 and through T. Spencer Knight Park, along the edge of the canal, to end at the visitor center on VanBuren Street.
- Turn around, and return to the start.

Date Enjoyed: _____

Notes:

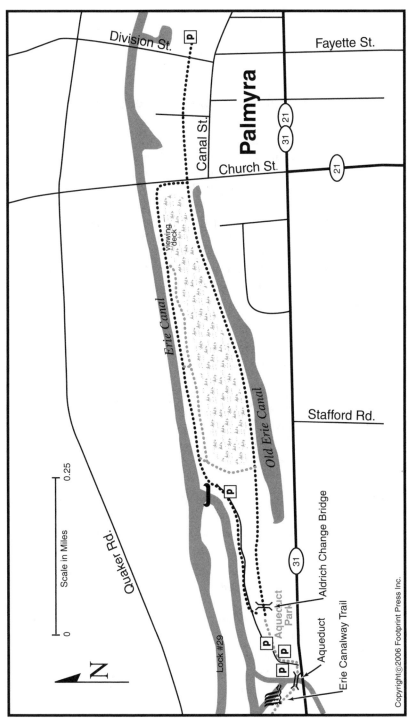

Erie Canalway Trail - Aqueduct Park

42.

Erie Canalway Trail — Aqueduct Park

Location:	Palmyra, Wayne County
Parking:	From Route 31, west of Palmyra, turn north into Aqueduct Park. Take the first right, and park near the Aldrich Change Bridge. N43º 03.842 - W77º 14.856
Alternative Parking:	Several other parking lots within Aqueduct Park, including one near the canoe launch. N43º 03.897 - W77º 14.657
Alternative Parking:	At Port of Palmyra Marina Park on Division Street. N43º 03.950 - W77º 13.762
Riding Time:	20 minutes round trip
Length:	2 miles round trip
Difficulty:	👟👟👟👟
Surface:	Stone dust and dirt trail
Trail Markings:	None
Uses:	🚶 🚴 🎿 🏃 ♿
Dogs:	Pets OK on leash
Contact:	NYS Canal Corp. PO Box 189, Albany, NY 12201-0189 1-800-422-6254 www.canals.state.ny.us

This trail is part of the Erie Canalway Trail that will some day span from Buffalo to Albany. It's currently the western end of an 85-mile segment that heads east through Rochester to Lockport. (See *Take Your Bike — Family Rides in the Rochester Area.*)

Settled in 1789 by John Swift, Palmyra was originally called Swift's Landing. Joseph Smith founded the Mormon Church here in 1830. Visitors by the thousands now converge on Palmyra each July for the Mormon's Hill Cumorah Pageant, the largest outdoor religious extravaganza in the United States.

The current Erie Canal flows through Palmyra's historic Aqueduct Park, named for the remains of the Palmyra Aqueduct, built in 1857 on the original Erie Canal to carry water over Ganargua Creek (also called Mud

The Aldrich Change Bridge, in the process of being restored.

The completed Aldrich Change Bridge, now
forever a part of the Erie Canalway Trail.

Creek). The home of Lock 29, Aqueduct Park offers picnic tables, swing sets, a small boat launch, restrooms, and parking. The park is open from 9 AM to 9 PM. Lock 29 is one of 6 locks in Wayne County, the most of any county in the state.

Also in Aqueduct Park, is the 144-year-old Aldrich Change Bridge. A change bridge allowed mules towing barges and packet boats along the canal to reverse directions without having to be unharnessed and transported across the canal. The 74-foot-long, 14-foot-wide bridge was built by Squire Whipple in 1858. It was an ingenious piece of engineering, especially for the time. Originally it sat over the canal in Rochester. In 1880 it was relocated to the enlarged canal near the border between Macedon and Palmyra. It collapsed into Mud Creek in 1996 during an ice storm, but it was hauled out and restored by volunteers over a 6-year period. It is the oldest surviving composite cast iron bridge in N.Y. State, and the only surviving canal change bridge. It now sits across the former canal bed which is filled in with soil and grass, a tribute to the original engineers and the volunteers who rescued this relic of our history.

From Aqueduct Park, the trail heads east over (or under) the Aldrich Change Bridge and follows the towpath of the Enlarged Erie Canal. On the loop back, you'll ride parallel to the current Erie Canal and pass a viewing dock, overlooking a pretty marsh area.

Trail Directions
- From the parking area near the Aldrich Change Bridge, head east, either over or under the change bridge.
- The Enlarged Erie Canal will appear on your right.
- Pass a trail to the left.
- Cross Church Street, another street, then Division Street before the trail ends in Port of Palmyra Marina Park.
- Turn around and return down the trail.
- After crossing Church Street, turn right on the dirt trail.
- Stop to enjoy the marsh view from the viewing deck.
- Stay right, along the canal, passing several side trails.
- You'll meet the park road near the canoe launch. Follow the park road back to your car.

Date Enjoyed: _____

Notes:

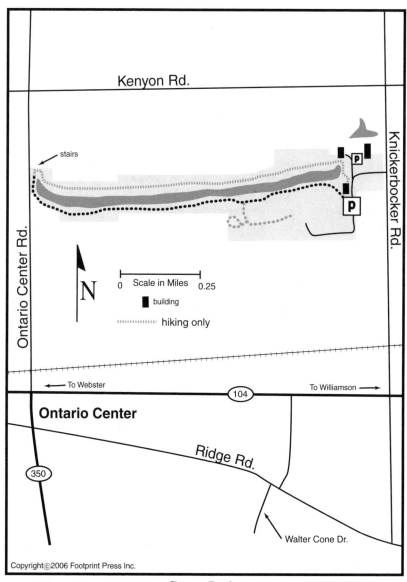

Casey Park

209

43.

Casey Park

Location:	Town of Ontario, Wayne County
Directions:	From Route 104 in Ontario, head north on Knicker-bocker Road, and watch left in 0.5 mile for Casey Park. Within the park, bear left to find the main parking lot, past the Ontario Parks and Recreation building. N43° 14.119 - W77° 17.310
Riding Time:	15 minutes round trip
Length:	2 miles round trip
Difficulty:	
Surface:	Dirt trail
Trail Markings:	None
Uses:	 south shore trail only
Dogs:	Pets OK on leash
Contact:	Town of Ontario Parks and Recreation Department 6551 Knickerbocker Road, Ontario, NY 14519 (315) 524-7447

The showcase of Casey Park is a long, narrow spring-fed lake that the trail loops around. The trail on the southern side of the lake is a flat, 8-foot-wide, tree-covered, packed-dirt trail that's suitable for bikes and wheelchairs, as well as hikers. As the trail rounds the western tip of the lake, it narrows and climbs up steps to the top of the spoilage pile hill that forms the northern shore. Starting here, the hiking-only trail is a narrow woods path that weaves up and down with the contours of the terrain, offering views of the lake below.

This park owes its existence to the geology and industrial history of Ontario. Between Ridge Road (Route 104) and Lake Ontario, a layer of iron ore crops out from below a ridge of limestone. The layer of limestone and iron continue south, but as they do, the dirt and rock on top become deeper and deeper. So, it's only around Ontario that the red-colored ore, called hematite, is economical to mine. The Ontario vein was discovered in 1811 by Mr. Knickerbocker as he dug a well to water his cattle.

Mining operations soon began using horses, dump carts, and a lot of manual labor. First, the men hauled away the dirt to reach the ore lying anywhere from 10 inches to 14 feet underground. A ball drill and blasting powder were used to break the ore into manageable chunks. It was then hauled by horse cart to a pier in Bear Creek harbor and loaded onto boats for shipment to Charlotte. In early mining operations, the dirt was filled back into the hole to leave an unmared landscape.

Eventually miners had to dig deeper and deeper. By the late 1880s steam shovels and steam locomotive trains were introduced. The area was dotted with mines (Moon Bed, Bean Bed, Wayne Ore Bed, Bundy Ore Bed, Hurley Bed, etc.) and with large blast furnace smelting operations. These operations dug deep pits that eventually filled with spring water, like the lake at Casey Park. And they left long, narrow mounds of rubble like the one under the Casey Lake's north rim hiking trail. Mining operations in the area ceased in the 1940s.

The Earl E. Casey Town Park began in 1964 with an initial purchase of 67 acres. It now encompasses 75 acres and offers a swim beach, canoe and paddle boat rental, ball fields, playground, restrooms, and trails. Biking is allowed on the south rim trail only.

Trail Directions
- From the parking area, cross the grass toward the lake and head west toward the woods, parallel to the lake.
- Although a few gravel trails to the left head back toward the active park area, continue along the water's edge.
- At the end of the lake, follow the water's edge around, until you meet the stairs.
- Turn around to return to the parking area.

Date Enjoyed: _____

Notes:

Definitions

Aqueduct: A stone, wood, or cement trough built to carry canal waters over an existing creek or river. At the time, the world's largest aqueduct was built in Rochester to span the Genesee River. Eleven stone arches were erected, spanning 800 feet, to withstand the annual floods of this wild river.

Ballast: Broken stone used as a base for a railroad bed.

Bog: An acid-rich, wet, poorly drained, spongy area characterized by plants such as sedges, heaths, and sphagnum.

Carding: Combing of wool.

Corduroy: A method of spanning a wet section of trail by laying logs perpendicular to the trail. This creates a bumpy effect like corduroy material.

Deciduous: Describes trees that loose their leaves in winter.

Drumlin: An elongated or oval hill created from glacial debris.

Esker: A ridge of debris formed when a river flowed under the glacier in an icy tunnel. Rocky material accumulated on the tunnel beds, and when the glacier melted, a ridge of rubble remained.

Feeder: A diverted stream, brook, or other water source used to maintain water the level in the canal.

Fulling Mill: A mill for cleaning wool and producing cloth.

Gristmill: A mill for grinding grain into flour.

Headrace: A trough or tunnel for conveying water to a point of industrial application.

Impoundments: Areas of marshland and ponds created by man-made earthen dikes.

Jewelweed: Also called touch-me-not, this plant is a member of the impatiens family. It grows in moist areas with a translucent stem and small snapdragon-like flowers in yellow, orange, or pink. The leaves shine silvery under water, hence the name jewelweed. The crushed plant has historically been used as a treatment for poison ivy, but recent studies show that it's not effective.

Lady's Slipper: This perennial herb has a pouch-like flower that resembles a dainty slipper. A victim of habitat destruction and over collection, this rare beauty is fast disappearing.

Leatherleaf: A shrub that grows on top of sphagnum moss and allows other plants to gain a foot hold. It produces white, bell-like flowers in spring.

Marsh: An area of soft, wet land.

Mule: The sterile offspring of a male donkey and a female horse. Mules were often used to pull boats along the Erie Canal.

Purple Loosestrife: An aggressive perennial carried from Europe in the ballast holds of ships. These blazing magenta flowering plants are spreading across American wetlands and crowding out native plants. The name is derived from the early practice of placing this plant over the yoke of quarrelsome oxen. The plant was said to help the oxen "loose their strife" or quiet down.

Sawmill: A mill for cutting trees into lumber.

Sphagnum Moss: A type of moss that grows in swamps and has an incredible capacity to hold water. It's estimated that this moss can soak up more than 100 times its own weight in water. In bogs where acids build up and oxygen is lacking, the moss compresses rather than degrades and forms peat. Dried, shredded, and packed in bales, sphagnum moss is sold as peat moss and is used by gardeners to retain moisture in soil.

Swamp: Wet, spongy land saturated and sometimes partially or intermittently covered with water.

Switchbacks: Winding the trail back and forth across the face of a steep area to make the incline more gradual.

Waste Weir: A dam along the side of a canal that allows overflow water to dissipate to a side waterway.

Trails Under 4 Miles

Page	Trail Name	Length (miles)
45	Kinney Creek Trail	1.5
188	Onondaga Lake Park Trails - Long Branch Park	1.5
181	Charlie Major Nature Trail	1.6
90	Frank J. Ludovico Sculpture Trail	1.7
52	Harriet Hollister - Big Oak/Bear Cub	1.9
188	Onondaga Lake Park Trails - Ten Eyck Drive	2.0
205	Erie Canalway Trail — Aqueduct Park	2.0
209	Casey Park	2.0
128	East Ithaca Recreation Way	2.2
52	Harriet Hollister - Fox/Racoon/Sidewinder	2.6
137	Shindagin Hollow State Forest	2.9
37	Dryer Road Park	3.0
192	Bear Trap Creek Bikeway	3.0
154	Auburn - Fleming Trail	3.2
26	Lehigh Crossing — Trolley Trail Loop	3.5

Trails 4 to 7 Miles

Page	Trail Name	Length (miles)
188	Onondaga Lake Park Trails - West Shore Trail	4.0
202	Erie Canalway Trail — Newark	4.2
120	Arnot Forest - Downhill	4.3
198	Old Erie Canal Lock 56 Trail	4.5
134	Ridgeway Trail	4.7
120	Arnot Forest - Loop	4.8
188	Onondaga Lake Park Trails - East Shore Trail	5.0
194	Canal Park Trailway	5.1
125	Cayuga Waterfront Trail	5.5
109	Catharine Valley Trail	6.0
130	South Hill Recreation Way	6.0
37	Dryer Road Park - Total	6 +
140	Hammond Hill State Forest	6.1
185	Spafford Forest	6.2
56	Stid Hill Multiple Use Area	6.5
63	Middlesex Valley Rail Trail	6.8
81	Keuka Lake Outlet Trail	6.8

Trails 7 – 11 Miles

Page	Trail Name	Length (miles)
150	Bear Swamp State Forest	7.2
59	Hi Tor Wildlife Management Area	7.4
30	Auburn Trail	7.5
144	Dryden Lake Park Trail	7.7
94	Sampson State Park — Lake Trail	7.8
99	Finger Lakes National Forest - Short	7.8
157	Howland Island	7.8
47	Canadice Lake Trail	8.1
176	Erie Canal Park	8.5
165	Hannibal - Hojack Trail	8.5
47	Canadice Lake Trail - Side Loops	9.0
77	Lakeshore Park / Seneca Lake State Park	9.0
116	Connecticut Hill Wildlife Management Area	9.1
169	Erie Canalway Trail (Port Byron to Jordan)	9.3
52	Harriet Hollister Spencer Memorial State Rec. Area	10.0
40	Hemlock Lake & Big Oaks Trails	10.1
173	Erie Canalway Trail (Jordan to Camillus)	10.8

Trails Over 11 Miles

Page	Trail Name	Length (miles)
140	Hammond Hill State Forest	11.0
188	Onondaga Lake Park Trails (total trails)	12.5
99	Finger Lakes National Forest - Medium	12.7
150	Bear Swamp State Forest (total trails)	13.0
161	Cato - Fair Haven Trail (Cayuga County Trail)	13.0
137	Shindagin Hollow State Forest (total trails)	18 +
68	Ontario Pathways	19.7
99	Finger Lakes National Forest - Long	25.1

1 Boot Trails

Page	Trail Name	Difficulty (boots)
30	Auburn Trail	1
45	Kinney Creek Trail	1
77	Lakeshore Park / Seneca Lake State Park	1
90	Frank J. Ludovico Sculpture Trail	1
125	Cayuga Waterfront Trail	1
134	Ridgeway Trail	1
144	Dryden Lake Park Trail	1
154	Auburn - Fleming Trail	1
173	Erie Canalway Trail (Jordan to Camillus)	1
176	Erie Canal Park	1
181	Charlie Major Nature Trail	1
188	Onondaga Lake Park Trails	1
192	Bear Trap Creek Bikeway	1
198	Old Erie Canal Lock 56 Trail	1
209	Casey Park	1

2 Boot Trails

Page	Trail Name	Difficulty (boots)
26	Lehigh Crossing — Trolley Trail Loop	2
40	Hemlock Lake & Big Oaks Trails	2
47	Canadice Lake Trail	2
68	Ontario Pathways	2
81	Keuka Lake Outlet Trail	2
107	Catharine Valley Trail	2
120	Arnot Forest - Downhill	2
128	East Ithaca Recreation Way	2
130	South Hill Recreation Way	2
161	Cato - Fair Haven Trail (Cayuga County Trail)	2
165	Hannibal - Hojack Trail	2
169	Erie Canalway Trail (Port Byron to Jordan)	2
202	Erie Canalway Trail — Newark	2
205	Erie Canalway Trail — Aqueduct Park	2

3 Boot Trails

Page	Trail Name	Difficulty (boots)
52	Harriet Hollister Spencer Memorial State Rec. Area	3
63	Middlesex Valley Rail Trail	3

3 Boot Trails

Page	Trail Name	Difficulty (boots)
94	Sampson State Park — Lake Trail	3
99	Finger Lakes National Forest - Short & Medium	3
150	Bear Swamp State Forest	3
157	Howland Island	3
185	Spafford Forest	3
194	Canal Park Trailway	3

4 Boot Trails

Page	Trail Name	Difficulty (boots)
37	Dryer Road Park	4
47	Canadice Lake Trail - Side Loops	4
56	Stid Hill Multiple Use Area	4
59	Hi Tor Wildlife Management Area	4
99	Finger Lakes National Forest - Long	4
116	Connecticut Hill Wildlife Management Area	4
120	Arnot Forest - Loop	4
137	Shindagin Hollow State Forest	4
140	Hammond Hill State Forest	4

Trails Where a Mountain Bike is Recommended

Page	Trail Name	Difficulty (boots)
37	Dryer Road Park	4
47	Canadice Lake Trail - Side Loops	4
52	Harriet Hollister Spencer Memorial State Rec. Area	3
56	Stid Hill Multiple Use Area	4
137	Shindagin Hollow State Forest	4
140	Hammond Hill State Forest	4
150	Bear Swamp State Forest	3

Paved Trails

Page	Trail Name	Difficulty (boots)
77	Lakeshore Park / Seneca Lake State Park	1
128	East Ithaca Recreation Way	1
188	Onondaga Lake Park Trails	1
193	Bear Trap Creek Bikeway	1

Loop Trails

Page	Trail Name	Difficulty (boots)
77	Lakeshore Park / Seneca Lake State Park	1
125	Cayuga Waterfront Trail	1
176	Erie Canal Park	1
181	Charlie Major Nature Trail	1
188	Onondaga Lake Park Trails - Long Branch Park & West Shore Trail	1
198	Old Erie Canal Lock 56 Trail	1
26	Lehigh Crossing — Trolley Trail Loop	2
40	Hemlock Lake & Big Oaks Trails	2
130	South Hill Recreation Way	2
52	Harriet Hollister Spencer Memorial State Rec. Area	3
94	Sampson State Park — Lake Trail	3
99	Finger Lakes National Forest - Short & Medium	3
150	Bear Swamp State Forest	3
157	Howland Island	3
185	Spafford Forest	3
59	Hi Tor Wildlife Management Area	4
99	Finger Lakes National Forest - Long	3
116	Connecticut Hill Wildlife Management Area	4
120	Arnot Forest - Loop	4
137	Shindagin Hollow State Forest	4
140	Hammond Hill State Forest	4
37	Dryer Road Park	4

Word Index

A

Aldrich Change Bridge: 207-208
Amita II: 199
Aqueduct: 167, 170-172, 174, 177-178, 206-208, 212
Arnot Forest: 120-124
Auburn and Rochester Railroad: 33
Auburn Trail: 26-29, 30-36
Auburn-Fleming Trail: 154-156

B

Bear Cub Trail: 52, 54
Bear Swamp State Forest: 150-153
Bear Trap Creek Bikeway: 192-193
Big Oak Trail: 52, 54
Big Oaks Trail: 40-44
Blazes: 12
Bloomer, Amelia: 91
Boots: 12

C

Canadice Lake: 41-42, 47-51, 53
Canadice Lake Trails: 47-51
Canal diggers: 91-92
Canal Park Trailway: 194-197
Canandaigua Corning Line: 71
Canandaigua Lake: 60, 61
Casey Park: 209-211
Cass Park: 125-127
Catharine Valley Trail: 107-115
Cato-Fair Haven Trail: 161-164
Cayuga and Susquehanna Railroad: 131
Cayuga Lake: 125-127
Cayuga Waterfront Trail: 125-127
Celerifere: 17
Change bridge: 206-208
Charlie Major Nature Trail: 181-184
Chemung Canal: 113
Chemung Railway: 113
Children: 22
City of Rochester Water Bureau: 41-43, 48-49

Clinton, DeWitt: 167
Cobblestone: 28, 32-34, 196
Colonial Belle: 199-200
Connecticut Hill Wildlife Management Area: 116-119
Corkscrew Railway: 84
Covered bridge: 121
Crooked Lake Canal: 83-84, 87

D

DaVinci, Leonardo: 17
De Sivrac: 17
Deer, white: 97
Delaware, Lackawanna, and Western Railroad: 131, 135
Difficulty (boots): 12
Dogs: 23
Domina, Susan: 8
Drumlins: 158, 163
Dry Dock: 198-200
Dryden Lake Park Trail: 144-147
Dryer Road Park: 37-39

E

Earl E. Casey Town Park: 209-211
Earll, Robert: 183-184
Earll, Tallman Distillery: 183
East Ithaca Recreation Way: 128-129
East Shore Recreation Trail: 188-191
Eddy, Mary Baker: 91
Erie Canal: 90-93, 157-158, 167-168, 194-197, 198-201, 202-204, 205-208
Erie Canal Park: 176-180
Erie Canal Parkway: 173-175
Erie Canalway Trail: 90-93, 169-172, 173-175, 176-180, 198-201, 202-204, 205-208
Erie Canalway Trail - Aqueduct Park: 205-208

Erie Canalway Trail - Jordan to Camillus: 173-175
Erie Canalway Trail - Newark: 202-204
Erie Canalway Trail - Port Byron to Jordan: 169-172
Ewers, Todd: 53

F

Fair Haven Beach State Park: 162
Finger Lakes National Forest: 99-106
Finger Lakes Trail: 138, 141
Fisher, Charles: 33
Fisher, J. Sheldon: 28, 33
Fotowerks, Ltd.: 2
Fox Run Trail: 52, 55
Frank J. Ludovico Sculpture Trail: 90-93
Freeman, Rich & Sue: 148

G

Ganondagan State Historic Site: 35, 38
Granger, John: 72

H

Haley, John: 191
Hammond Hill State Forest: 140-143
Hanna, David: 92
Hannibal-Hojack Trail: 161, 165-166
Harriet Hollister Spencer Memorial State Recreation Area: 52-55
Hawley, Jesse: 167
Helmet: 21
Hematite: 210
Hemlock Lake: 40-44, 48-49
Hemlock Lake Trail: 40-44
Heron rookery: 65
Hi Tor Wildlife Management Area: 59-62, 65
History: 17-18

Hobby horse: 17
Hoffman, Ed: 113
Hojack Rail System: 165
Honeoye Lake: 53-54
Howland Island: 157-160
Hunting: 10, 65, 101, 159
Hurricane Agnes: 71, 73, 84

I

Iron ore: 210-211
Iroquois Confederacy: 78
Iroquois Indians: 102, 113-114

J

John Haley Memorial West Shore Trail: 188-191

K

Kendaia: 95
Keuka Lake: 82
Keuka Lake Outlet Trail: 81-88
Kinney Creek Trail: 45-46

L

Lake Trail: 94-98
Lakeshore Park: 77-80
Lakeside Paper Company: 183
Lanning, Jonathan: 97
Lehigh Crossing Park: 26-29, 33
Lehigh Valley Rail Trail: 65
Lehigh Valley Railroad: 33, 35, 43, 65, 127,145, 163
Lehigh Valley Trail: 26-29, 33, 35
Lincoln, Abraham: 72
Lock: 198-201
Long Branch Park: 188-191
Ludovico, Frank J.: 90-93
Lynch, Michael: 2

M

MacMillan, Kirkpatrick: 17
Major, Charles T. Jr.: 182, 184
Markers: 13
Michaux, Ernest: 17
Middlesex Valley Rail Trail: 63-67
Milestones: 33
Mills: 33, 82-88, 183-184

Montour, Catharine: 113-114
Mormon: 206
Mottville Factories & Mills: 183
Museum: 28, 98, 177-178, 191
N
New York Central Railroad: 28, 33, 73, 84
Newfield Bridge: 121
O
Old Erie Canal Lock 56 Trail: 198-201
Olenick, Andy: 2
Onondaga Lake Park Trails: 188-191
Ontario Pathways: 68-76
P
Penn Central Corporation: 71, 73
Penn Yan and New York Railway Company: 84
Pfieffer, Brain: 92
Phelps, Oliver III: 72
Pumphouse: 28, 32-34
Pusmucans, Wilhelmina: 92
R
Racks: 24
Racoon Run: 52, 55
Red House Country Inn B&B: 102
Ridgeway Swamp: 134-136
Ridgeway Trail: 134-136
Rochester & Eastern Rapid Railway: 28
Rochester Bicycling Club: 57-58
Rochester Water Bureau: 41-42, 49
Rookery: 65
S
Sampson Naval Training Station: 95
Sampson State Park: 94-98
Sampson, Rear Admiral William T.: 96
Sculpture Trail: 90-93

Seneca Indians: 95
Seneca Lake: 77-80, 82, 94-98
Seneca Lake State Park: 77-80
Seneca Mill: 83, 86
Seneca Trail: 26-29
Sheridan, John: 86
Shindagin Hollow State Forest: 137-139
Sibley, Mark: 72
Sidewinder Trail: 52, 55
Sims' Store: 177
Skaneateles Paper Company: 183
South Hill Recreation Way: 130-133
Southern Central Railroad: 145
Spafford Forest: 185-187
Starley, James: 18
Stid Hill Multiple Use Area: 56-58
Swift, John: 206
T
Telarico, Hyon: 92
Ten Eyck Drive: 188-191
Thompson, R.W.: 17
Trolley Trail: 26-29, 33
Tunnel: 33, 34, 79
U
Uses: 13
V
Vanderbilt, Cornelius: 33
Velocipede: 17-18
Victor Hiking Trails: 27, 31-32
von Drais, Baron Karl: 17
W
Washington, George: 118
Water tower: 72, 76
Weed, Edward & Elihu: 171
West Shore Trail: 188-191
Willow Glen: 183
Willseyville Swamp: 134-136
Wilson, Jared: 72

Other Books Available from Footprint Press, Inc.

Cross-country Skiing and Snowshoeing:

> *Snow Trails – Cross-country Ski and Snowshoe in Central and Western NY*
> ISBN# 0-9656974-52   U.S. $16.95
> 80 mapped locations for winter fun on skis or snowshoes.

Hiking:

> *200 Waterfalls in Central & Western New York - A Finders' Guide*
> ISBN#1-930480-01-6   U.S. $18.95
> Discover over 200 wondrous waterfalls.

> *Peak Experiences – Hiking the Highest Summits in NY, County by County*
> ISBN# 0-9656974-01   U.S. $16.95
> A guide to reaching the highest point in each county of New
> York State.

> *Take A Hike! Family Walks in the Rochester Area*
> ISBN# 0-9656974-79   U.S. $16.95
> 60 day hikes within a 15-mile radius of Rochester, N.Y.

> *Take A Hike! Family Walks in the Finger Lakes & Genesee Valley Region*
> ISBN# 0-9656974-95   U.S. $16.95
> 51 day hike trails throughout central and western New York.

> *Take A Hike – Family Walks in New York's Finger Lakes Region*
> ISBN# 1-930480-20-2   U.S. $19.95
> 2nd edition - 68 day-hike trails in the Finger Lakes Region.

> *Bruce Trail – An Adventure Along the Niagara Escarpment*
> ISBN# 0-9656974-36   U.S. $16.95
> Learn the secrets of backpackers on a five-week hike in Ontario,
> Canada, as they explore the abandoned Welland Canal routes,
> caves, ancient cedar forests, and white cobblestone beaches
> along Georgian Bay.

> *Backpacking Trails of Central & Western New York State*
> ISBN# none   U.S. $2.00
> A 10-page booklet describing the backpackable trails of
> central and western NYS with contact information to obtain
> maps and trail guides.

Bird Watching:

> *Birding in Central & Western New York – Best Trails &*
> *Water Routes for Finding Birds*
> ISBN# 1-930480-00-8   U.S. $16.95
> 70 of the best places to spot birds on foot, from a car,
> or from a canoe.

Bicycling:

Take Your Bike! Family Rides in the Rochester Area
ISBN# 1-930480-02-4   U.S. $18.95
Converted railroad beds, paved bike paths, and woods trails combine to create the 42 safe bicycle adventures within an easy drive of Rochester, N.Y.

Take Your Bike! Family Rides in the Finger Lakes & Genesee Valley Region
ISBN# 0-9656974-44   U.S. $16.95
Converted railroad beds, woods trails, and little-used country roads combine to create the 40 safe bicycle adventures through central and western New York State.

Explore History:

Cobblestone Quest - Road Tours of New York's Historic Buildings
ISBN# 1-930480-19-9   U.S. $19.95
17 self-guided tours for observing the history and diversity of unique cobblestone buildings that are found within a 65-mile radius of Rochester, NY, and nowhere else. Enjoy the tours by car, motorcycle, or bicycle.

Canoeing & Kayaking:

Take a Paddle - Western New York Quiet Water for Canoes & Kayaks
ISBN# 1-930480-23-7   U.S. $18.95
Offering over 250 miles of flat-water creeks and rivers, and 20 ponds and lakes, this guide provides a fun way to explore Western New York.

Take a Paddle - Finger Lakes New York Quiet Water for Canoes & Kayaks
ISBN# 1-930480-24-5   U.S. $18.95
Offering over 370 miles of flat-water creeks and rivers, and 35 ponds and lakes, this guide provides a fun way to explore the beautiful Finger Lakes region.

Self-help:

Alter – A Simple Path to Emotional Wellness
ISBN# 0-9656974-87   U.S. $16.95
A self-help manual that assists in recognizing and changing emotional blocks and limiting belief systems, using easy-to-learn techniques of biofeedback to retrieve subliminal information and achieve personal transformation.

For sample maps and chapters explore web site:
www.footprintpress.com

Yes, I'd like to order Footprint Press books:

#

_____	*Take A Hike! Family Walks in New York's Finger Lakes*	$19.95
_____	*Take Your Bike! Family Rides in New York's Finger Lakes*	$19.95
_____	*200 Waterfalls in Central & Western NY*	$18.95
_____	*Take a Paddle - Western NY*	$18.95
_____	*Take a Paddle - Finger Lakes NY*	$18.95
_____	*Cobblestone Quest*	$19.95
_____	*Peak Experiences—Hiking the Highest Summits of NY*	$16.95
_____	*NYS County Summit Club patch*	$2.00
_____	*Snow Trails—Cross-country Ski & Snowshoe*	$16.95
_____	*Birdng in Central & Western NY*	$16.95
_____	*Take A Hike! Family Walks in the Rochester Area*	$16.95
_____	*Take A Hike! Family Walks in the Finger Lakes & Genesee Valley*	$16.95
_____	*Take Your Bike! Family Rides in the Rochester Area*	$18.95
_____	*Take Your Bike! Family Rides in the Finger Lakes & Genesee Valley*	$16.95
_____	*Bruce Trail—Adventure Along the Niagara Escarpment*	$16.95
_____	*Backpacking Trails of Central & Western NYS*	$2.00
_____	*Alter—A Simple Path to Emotional Wellness*	$16.95

Sub-total:	$_____
FL State and Canadian residents add 7% tax:	$_____
Shipping & handling:	$ 3.00
Total enclosed:	$_____

Your Name: _____

Address: _____

City: _____ State (Province): _____

Zip (Postal Code): _____ Country: _____

Make check payable and mail to:
Footprint Press, Inc.
303 Pine Glen Court
Englewood, FL 34223

Or order through web site: **www.footprintpress.com**